A FEW BIG IDEAS

Hope you
enjoy!
Beech

Happy Reading!

A FEW BIG IDEAS

TO GROW YOUR BUSINESS

STEVE BEECHAM
WITH MARK BRADLEY

BOOKLOGIX®
Alpharetta, Georgia

Although the author and publisher have made every effort to ensure that the information in this book was correct at the time of first publication, the author and publisher do not assume and hereby disclaim any liability to any party for any loss, damage, or disruption caused by errors or omissions, whether such errors or omissions result from negligence, accident, or any other cause.

Copyright © 2024 by Steve Beecham

All rights reserved. No part of this book may be reproduced or transmitted in any form or by any means, electronic or mechanical, including photocopying, recording, or any information storage and retrieval system, without permission in writing from the author.

ISBN: 978-1-6653-0792-5 - Paperback
eISBN: 978-1-6653-0793-2 - eBook

These ISBNs are the property of BookLogix for the express purpose of sales and distribution of this title. The content of this book is the property of the copyright holder only. BookLogix does not hold any ownership of the content of this book and is not liable in any way for the materials contained within. The views and opinions expressed in this book are the property of the Author/Copyright holder, and do not necessarily reflect those of BookLogix.

Library of Congress Control Number: 2023923725

Printed in the United States of America

⊚This paper meets the requirements of ANSI/NISO Z39.48-1992 (Permanence of Paper)

Cover Design by Jeff Gribble, Industry Communications

012224

CONTENTS

Introduction	VII
Steve's Story	VIII
Mark's Story	IX
Top 100	1
A–G	4
Local Politics	6
Life Purpose	9
New in Sales	15
Hobbies	17
Kids	19
Creating New Habits	22
Mayor of Your Village 1	25
Mayor of Your Village 2	28
Mayor of Your Village 3	31
A-List	34
Constant and Consistent Advertising	36
Go Deep	38
Direct Connect	42
Hang Out Where the Money Is	44
WOW	46
You Are the Average of Your Five Best Friends	48
Personal Not Professional	50
Bring Your Assets, Not Your Agenda	52
Cloud Referrals	55
Community Organizations	57
Events	59
Paint Better Pictures	61
Dinner Parties	64
Farming	66
FORD and HEFE	69
Grow Your Referrals	71
Sales Pitch	75
Video	77
Points System	79
BUZZ	81
Be Santas Claus	83
Newsletter	85

Join More Clubs!	88
Levels of Introduction	90
Small Groups	92
Visiting	94
Who Can I Introduce You To?	96
Breakroom Sticky	98
Hometown Monopoly	100
Make a List	101
Employee Appreciation Day	102
Be Curious Like a Ten-Year-Old	103
Create Your Own Club	106
Outside Looking In	108
Google Reviews/Testimonials	110
Referrals	111
Are You Good Enough?	114
Circle the Wagons	117
Own Your Own Backyard	119
Spoke and Hub	123
Buying Leads	126
The Tapes You Play in Your Head	128
Three Things Expert Salespeople Do	132
Time Management	134
Entrepreneurship	136
You Can't Grow If You Don't Let Go	140
R&D 1	143
R&D 2	146
R&D 3	149
R&D 4	150
Passions	151
Increase Your Prices	153
Hiring	155
I Believe	156
Mentoring: The Greatest Way to Give Back Your Knowledge	158
Praise	161
Mini Me	162
Fear	163
Bottles and Brainstorming	165
Board of Directors	166
Go Pro in Your Sport	168
Top 100 – For Life	171
Make It Happen	172

Introduction

I get hired to give motivational speeches to insurance agents, mortgage loan-officers, financial advisors, and retail owners. Whoever hires me usually has an agenda they are trying to promote to their employees. They have a message they want to get across to their troops.

But I always wonder, what do the troops want to hear? If I were in that audience, I would want a nugget to take away. Something I could apply today to help my business.

This book is meant to be that nugget.

I have been working on this book for over ten years and it is crazy how these ideas stick.

I want to teach you the ideas I've learned from some of the top salespeople and smartest business owners in the country. I created a whole series of fifty marketing ideas. These Ideas can change your income or change your life today.

I read the book, Who Not How, and a light bulb went on. I hate to write, and failed English class, but who do I know can take these ideas and concepts and put them in a book? Who do I know would see this as fun?

Mark Bradley. He has twenty-two years of experience in the real estate industry. He also has a minor degree in journalism and has been published in several different periodicals throughout his career. He asked if he could help, and I took him up on it.

Steve's Story

Several years ago, my mortgage company tripled in size. I went from about five loan officers to over twenty in one month. The problem was I had a bunch of new salespeople and I didn't do any advertising. All my business came from referrals. Some of these salespeople were used to buying leads and doing traditional radio/newspaper/mailer-type advertising. I needed to start holding sales meetings and I needed to teach them my techniques for building a referral business. If I didn't, they might not survive at our company. I came up with fifty-two marketing Ideas as a playbook to be used to learn a new strategy every week. Hopefully, you can use these strategies in your business, and it will improve your referral business.

Over the last thirty years, I have owned several businesses. Some of the businesses were successful, some of them not so successful. I've been in sales for most of my life. Sometimes, I have done well, and other times not so well! I've spent the last twenty or thirty years really trying to figure out why some people are more successful. I've interviewed them, studied them, and read a lot of books.

I came up with a concept that I call Bass-Ackward Business. In other words, you can help people and not hustle them to get more business.

If you're tired of cold calling people, buying leads, or going to Chamber of Commerce meetings and handing out your business cards, this is for you.

Mark's Story

Mark started his business career in 1997 and has been a top-producing realtor, team leader, managing broker, trainer, coach, and is now the principal broker of his own brokerage. Prior to owning a real estate brokerage, he owned and operated a regional drayage operation in four states. He has been appointed to multiple charity boards and held several leadership positions.

His mantra has always been to under promise and over deliver to his clients. He developed a servant attitude in his business several years ago.

His customers come from his sphere of influence and past clients. That is the way he prefers it. "It's more fun to work with people who know and like you," he says. He incorporates many of the ideas in this book into his everyday business and coaches his agents in these principles.

His guarantee is, if this book doesn't help you or give you an idea you can implement, He will give you your money back.

He wants you to grow your business in your community. He wants you to create more sales. He wants people to call you and say, "Hey, man, how can I spend money with you?" That's the whole concept. That's the way he wants every deal to come.

So, read a chapter every week and start changing the way you get business.

Top 100

Everybody wants a nugget they can put in their pocket and use right away. The "Top 100" is such a nugget. If you do this, we promise you will get more business.

Do you have a list of the top 100 people who could change your life this year? Most people know they need to make calls and meet more potential customers. They know somebody needs to buy their product. But they don't know who they should call or who they want to call.

What if you sat down and made a list of people who are not direct hits? If you are a mortgage guy like me, a direct hit is a real estate agent. If you are a financial guy, a direct hit is a wealthy person. If you are an insurance guy, a direct hit is a person who owns a successful business and has a lot of kids driving cars. But what happens if you go after the indirect hits? People who are influential in your community and could introduce you to direct hits. If you can meet these 100 people this year, and if three or four of those people bought your product, it could change your life. Or, if three or four of those people introduced you to people who would buy your product, one of these people could buy ten times more than what you are selling now. But you never even thought to have a conversation with them.

Let's put together a list that says, "These Top 100 people can change your life this year." They can change the amount of money you make. They can help you grow your business. They can change the introductions to people that you meet. But you have to build that list of the Top 100.

Now, you can't eat the elephant all at one time. So, you have to take it in small bites, right? But, one of the things you can do

A FEW BIG IDEAS   1

is take 100 and divide it by ten or twelve months. Use the list on the following page to write down 100 businesspeople you need to meet who you do not know or read the chapters under "R&D." The key is to have a list.

It blows me away that when I go to coach someone, even in small towns in America, how few people they know in their community. I remember being in a small town in the South and talking to this gentleman about his business. On the way into town, I purposely looked at businesses. I thought they were pretty good sized, so I wrote them down.

My client grew up in this town and thought he knew everyone. I asked him who ran those businesses, and he only knew the answer to five of fifteen. I said, "Dude, you need to meet those people you don't know. Surely you know somebody that works there or something about the owner, but have you ever sat down and talked to that owner? Have you ever had lunch with them to talk to them about your financial business, or about how you can bring value to their business? They look to be significant businesses for this size town."

Just look out your back door! I was coaching the hairstylist who actually rents the space next door to me. I asked, "Have you actually gone out and walked around and introduced yourselves to any of the businesspeople in our area? I mean, just in walking distance of your office."

They replied, "No, we have never done that."

I said, "Best I can tell, people in offices and retail stores need haircuts. Why wouldn't you just introduce yourself?"

Wouldn't you think that if there were businesses around you, with at least one hundred people working at them, maybe one or two of those people might be willing to walk across the street to get their hair done because it's convenient? But they do not know you're there, because you never made that connection. You've never gone over there and spoken to them.

And don't you think that the hairstylist, as they drive to work every day, could write down the names of the businesses they pass? If you can meet some of these businesses in the next couple of months, you could put these people on your Top 100 who could possibly change your life.

So, start making a list of the Top 100 people who could change your life this year. When you do, start by thinking about the obvious ones.

- Mayor and city council
- School principals
- Your child's teacher
- Owner of your favorite restaurants
- County Commissioners, state representatives, senators, governor
- Owners and employees of the companies you write checks to
- Your neighbors
- Everyone in your club
- Your pastor
- Owner where you buy your plants and hardware
- Car repair shop
- A business you ride by on the way to work
- The largest employer in town
- Your kid's employers and coaches
- Painter, plumber, electrician, and HVAC owners
- Church members

All these people know people you need to meet. All of these people have sent me business over the years. I'm not meeting them to sell them something, I meet them to see how I can get them more business!

You have to have a list of the Top 100.

Bonus: Once you meet your Top 100, then create a Top 100 for life. Who would be the coolest people in your world you want to meet? See chapter, "Top 100 – For Life." Additionally, write down *your* Top 100 in the notes section at the end of this book.

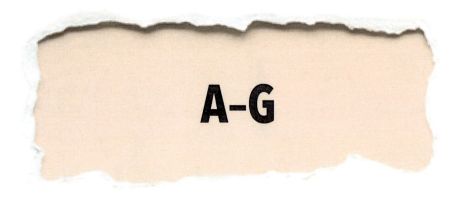

A-G

When I started in the mortgage industry, business was slow. One day, I walked down the hall to my mentor and fellow loan officer, Ed Wheeler's, office. I asked Ed if he was slow, and he said he was. I asked him for some words of wisdom. He said in a previous business he had been in, the guy he worked for taught him this marketing technique and Ed used it all the time and it worked.

In the old days, we kept customer contact information on a Rolodex. It was arranged in alphabetical order and there was a card for everyone. Under "B," you could find Steve Beecham and you could write on the card, my phone number, and other pertinent information. The more contacts you had, the bigger the Rolodex. Lots of people had more than one Rolodex. The old boss told him that when it got slow, just pull out your Rolodex and start calling people. Start with "A" and if you called everyone in your Rolodex, you wouldn't get to "G" before somebody would call you about a deal. Most of the time, it was not somebody you were talking to but the "Mortgage Gods smiled on you" if you were doing a marketing task. Just the task of getting in touch with people for any reason was enough to get some business going again.

This is the basis for my whole marketing program today. I just call people! I call around twenty people a day, every weekday. It is free and easy. You can do it when you are slow or on your way to work or home.

We all have a computer and a phone with contacts, and they are arranged in alphabetical order. You can do the same thing. I did it so much that I had to add a twist. If I called starting with "A" all the time, I would never reach "Z." One day, I just started adding everyone in my database on my calendar. I assigned a time to call that person. Now, I randomly call people all over my database every day and not in alphabetical order.

You can learn all about how I do it in the "Mayor of Your Village" chapter.

Prior to getting into the mortgage business, I owned a men's and women's clothing store. An older merchant, who became my mentor in that business, suggested I buy a card filing system. The system was like the Rolodex, but it had a place to record what size the person was in every category: shoes, jacket, waist, pants, etc. That way you could call Mr. Jones and suggest he come by and look at the new suit you had in his size. Then, when they bought, you could record what they bought like a navy blazer and khaki pants. Then, when a new tie or shirt came in, that would complement that navy blazer and khaki pants, you could call him and have him come see it. This was a cool way of letting the customer know you knew what they needed.

I adopted some of that in the mortgage business. I now keep up with important information on the customer. I have the interest rate they currently have—in case there is a lower rate I need to call them about. I have their hobbies listed so I can introduce them to others with the same hobby. I also log in their spouse and kids' names as well as where they work and what it is, specifically, they do in that job. I have found this to be very helpful when I call them. It gives me the information I need to carry on a conversation about personal stuff as well as professional stuff.

Also, have their birthday information. Send them a card with a Starbucks or Chick-fil-A gift card. And always, always call them on their special day. They love it that you remembered!

Mark says he keeps track of his calls with a good CRM (customer relationship management) system. He uses Commissions, Inc. But there are many other CRM platforms available for your use. Most of them are industry-specific so do your research before making a purchase. You can set reminders for birthdays, calls, appointments, etc. Most of them will link to your Gmail or Outlook calendars.

Have a system in place to time block your daily calls. If it's not on your calendar, it doesn't happen.

Local Politics

Are you trying to figure out how you can meet *more people in your community?*

Are you trying to figure out how you can build deeper relationships with people? Specifically, people that can do business with you?

Are you trying to figure out who could introduce you to great prospects?

Several years ago, I stumbled on one of the best things that's ever happened to me. I call it Local Politics.

What people don't understand is that your local politician is a person who's decided they need to know everyone in town. I noticed that people who were in business would not go knock on anyone's door and ask them for business. They were too scared to do that. They wouldn't ask them to "come to my restaurant" or "let me do your legal services" or "let me be your accountant." But what they would do is if they ran for office like city council, they would put on their running shoes on a Saturday and go door to door in as many subdivisions as they could. And they would knock on the door and say, "Vote for me." Most people wouldn't go up and ask for your business. That's too scary for them, but if they're running for office, they don't have a problem asking you to vote for them and asking you to give them money for their campaign.

So, I said, "You know, maybe I need to tap into politics a little bit." One time, a friend of mine was running for city council, and I gave him one hundred dollars. Next thing you know, I'm invited to a political rally at someone's house.

Now I'm in a person's house with all his friends and neighbors.

And my politician friend is introducing me to everyone because I gave him money and told him I would support him. All I did was give him $100 and he introduced me to everyone at the party. How could you get a warmer introduction to a stranger than that?

Then, I found out that it not only works on the local city level. It works on the county level and even the state level. I started giving to county commissioners and state representatives and senators. They invited me to their campaign parties and introduced me to their friends. The best part is most of the people who participate are very well connected. These are the influencers in your community. These people really care and a lot of them are highly successful people. Those are the people I want to know.

I started throwing parties for people who were running for office that I liked. I have parties at my house and invite a bunch of people.

Now, anytime I need a favor or an introduction, I call a politician and say, "Hey, do you know so and so?" And if they do, they make the phone call for me. They meet me for lunch. They do anything in the world to help me meet that person. If you're not using politics to meet people in your local village, you need to consider it. It's not expensive. I thought I had to write big checks. But no, you don't have to write big checks. All you need to do is write small checks, write a check based on whatever your belief is and how much you can spend.

Start using politics as a way to meet new people. Politicians consistently are having parties in neighborhoods to try to meet folks in those neighborhoods and they'll invite you to come. Think about who you know locally that may be running for office. A person that believes what you believe. Go call them and ask to get involved.

You can get involved in politics in many ways. The main reason is to help the candidate achieve success. You could be a caller at a phone bank. They need people to call other people in the community. You can volunteer to call your friends and say, "Hey, my buddy John is running for city council. I'd love for you to meet him." Ask if it would be okay for the candidate to call them. You can also volunteer to put up yard signs. People will tell the candidate they will put up a sign and you just go do it for them. While at the person's house or office introduce yourself.

What I do with politicians is I ask them, "Who can I introduce you to?" There are certain people in the community they are familiar with but might not know personally. They'd like to meet these people because they are influencers in their neighborhood. Maybe there's someone that's known to give money to campaigns. They also know who votes. They have a list of everybody who voted in the last election and how they voted; Republican, Democrat, or whatever. They know that those are significant people for them to meet because they are more likely to vote again.

So, if they don't know them, they *want* to know them. Quite often, I'll do a thing I'll teach you in a later chapter called "Visiting." I'll put up somebody that's running for office in my car and I'll drive him around and introduce him to everybody. I know people that live in the area they're running in. Politics is a great way to get out and meet a lot of new people. Unfortunately it only comes every two to four years, but during that time period, if you use it wisely, you can meet a large group of new, cool people.

My friend Joe decided to run for mayor of our town. Joe was not the handpicked candidate by "the powers that be," but had decided to put his hat in the race. On the weekends, I would pick Joe up and we would ride around to people's houses and I would introduce him to the people I knew. Joe came up with the idea to get his tractor out and create a hayride around neighborhoods and let the kids ride on the tractor. He got to meet the parents because they came out to see what was going on. He will tell you that because he used this marketing technique, and the fact that I introduced him to so many people, it helped him win.

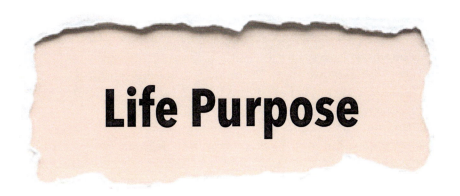

Life Purpose

Discovering your life purpose is the most important *thing you can do for your business and your personal life.*

Your life purpose is different than your passion. Passion is what you do for fun—like a hobby—but purpose is what you are put on this planet to do. Purpose is about your calling or your superpower. I'm passionate about riding my motorcycle, but my life purpose is to "Help others get from where they are to where they want to go."

When you discover your life purpose, you have a different reason for doing what you do. The job you have is just the instrument you use to fulfill your purpose, not the purpose itself.

Your PURPOSE is about OTHERS, not YOU!
Your PURPOSE is about your UNIQUE ABILITIES!
Your PURPOSE is not DEPENDENT on OTHERS!
When discovering your purpose, ask yourself:

WHAT DO MY FRIENDS AND FAMILY CALL ON ME FOR?
WHAT AM I WILLING TO FIGHT FOR?

Let's step through events in your life that can help you determine your life purpose.

Family

What are the characteristics of your family?

Some families are high-strung and some are laid back. Some are athletic and some are movie critics. Take a look at your family from an outside view of its unique characteristics.

What personality did they give you? Maybe you are the one who everyone calls on to tell a joke or you may be the family shrink. Sometimes, you run from the behavior and sometimes we are very similar to them. The key is to understand what personality your family has given you.

My family is full of talkers and listeners. They are builders and politicians. Southern and churchy. My family has always been very involved in helping others. My dad loves teaching Sunday School. This has made me more extroverted, interested in building things, and politically involved.

Case in point, my friend Barbara Duffy is the executive director of a nonprofit. Her family was instrumental in helping her find her purpose. In her family, there was always a conversation about taking the gifts you have and helping other people with your gifts. She took that purpose and helped create North Fulton Community Charities.

Town

The town you grew up in has created unique things about you. Basically, it was an environment that shaped you. People in your town view you in a certain way. People in your high school classes had opinions about you.

I went to elementary school in North Augusta, South Carolina. Since my dad was in medical school, we lived in a blue-collar working-class neighborhood. This was during school segregation and I lived in a racially mixed neighborhood, which shaped my understanding of what it's like to be African American living in the South. I was successful in school and in sports. Then, we moved to Roswell, Georgia to start high school and I was the new kid. I saw how hard it was to be accepted and to succeed. This made me more needy and wanting to be accepted in my new town, which in turn made me more outgoing and able to get out of my comfort zone.

My friend Ralph Rucker has owned a lot of businesses. He knows a lot of wealthy and philanthropic people in the community. He says his purpose is to help those in need who don't have a voice or don't have an advocate. We sat down and decided to start Ralph's Angels. He calls wealthy women in the community to help him with projects. They are his angels. Ralph's Angels.

Life

Think about where you went to high school and college. The fraternities and sororities and the independents you knew and associated with. The cars you drove as well as the clothing you wore. All the jobs you had and the people you met through them. Think about the skills you learned and the things you didn't like with all the jobs you had.

My first job was selling cars and I learned that car salesmen do not always tell the truth. Then, I opened a clothing store where I learned about inventory control and marketing to my community. After that, I got into the garbage business and discovered that some people could work cheaper than me because they had less overhead. Then I discovered the mortgage business and found I was good at understanding real estate and finance even though I have never balanced my checkbook.

I took those skills and experiences and started writing books and speaking. All of that taught me how to be successful and how to lose it all!

My wife, Mary Beecham, is actively involved in what I call the Tar Baby. King's Ridge Christian School is where she is all-in, with both hands and feet stuck in the King's Ridge Tar Baby. She feels it is her purpose to see this newer school from start-up to full enrollment. She contributes by being there to help others who are in positions of inspiration. Her job is to support them and tell others in the community about the school. The school motto, "To Know, To Serve, To Believe" is important to who she is. She believes that the community needs a school with that mission. She has turned her life purpose into a career.

Ron Clark went to work by accident because he needed a job, and the school needed a teacher. He saw that his purpose was to bring excitement to the kids about learning. He had the ability to dream "what if?" He discovered that kids were most vulnerable in middle school. He believed they could really rise to the challenge of excellence like he had always done. He convinced his students to write a letter to President Clinton, asking if they could go sleep in the White House. He went on to find the Ron Clark Academy in Atlanta, Georgia—a nonprofit private middle school with a vision to transform learning methods for students and teaching techniques for teachers.

Let's Break Down Purpose

You must discover your purpose from forty thousand feet. Look at your family, job, and life experiences, and from forty thousand feet think about what they leaned on you to do. What they called on you for in a time of need. Then think about the following life purposes: helping, fixing, problem-solving, inventing, organizing, managing, coaching, accounting, and teaching. Start with these. Then add your strengths: communicator, speaker, connector, empathizer, and listener.

When you put these two together it looks like this:

I talk to people to help them solve problems. I teach people how to fix things. I love coaching people on how to connect with others.

Now, it is time to combine your strengths into your specific purpose. What is your superpower that gets you fired up? One that you want to do because it makes you feel better? Something you would talk to people about and not worry about making any money?

Then add the KICKER. Put a little something at the end of the purpose that drives you. One thing that sends you to a place that is endless and bigger than you. A KICKER is a few words that define it very specifically. I help people. But what do I specifically help them with? I don't want to help someone in a car accident. I don't want to help someone balance their checkbook. I want to help them *get from where they are now to where they want to go.*

I don't want to help someone discover a pyramid or a treasure. I want to help them get off drugs or kick a soccer ball better.

I don't want to coach someone to be a better driver or a better writer. I want to coach someone on how to have a better relationship with their spouse or child.

You need to always add the kicker, so you are very tuned in. When you are tuned into your purpose, then an amazing thing happens. You don't wait to be called to a problem, you just find that the problem finds you. It may be the person next to you at lunch or the seat next to you on a plane. It's like you become an angel to others. You were just there when they needed you.

SECRET—If you have purpose and you look for it in your day, you will always be happy. Purpose does that for you. When I found this, I was not really enjoying the mortgage business at that time. Business was terrible and I was ready to give up. Then, I discovered my purpose and now I see my mortgage business as a widget that I use to live a more purposeful life. When someone comes into my mortgage world, I view them through a different lens. The lens I see is someone who is living *here*, but they want to live *there*. So, I help them get from where they are to where they want to go. This is my purpose. When I speak or hold workshops, it's the same thing. People are struggling with their businesses and need information on how to get from where they are in business to where they want to go.

Ask yourself these questions:

WHAT'S NOT GOING TO GET DONE IF I DON'T DO IT?
WHAT HAS BROUGHT YOU GREAT JOY IN INTERACTING WITH OTHERS?
We all want to answer the question, "WHAT DOES THIS ALL MEAN?"

Marianne Williamson says your job is separate from the rest of your life and you are looking for a CALLING or purpose to finish out your life. The calling gives your soul the ability to serve others with your gifts.

We all want to connect with something deeply and intimately.
We want to have the power of choice in our lives.
We want to know we are appreciated.
What is our calling? We all have one.

Ultimately, it ends up being that special thing we have to give to others we meet. The giving of our knowledge and love to others is what it is all about. "Be Santa Claus" all year round.

Through our inner growth and discovery of purpose, we end up connecting deeply with our community. When we do, the community talks about us and the effect we have had on them. This turns into a positive buzz about our true desire to help and that turns into more opportunities to give. We typically make more money by being the go-to person for other's needs.

If you are new in sales, I believe there are three *things you HAVE TO DO.*

1. You must believe *YOU ARE GOOD ENOUGH.* Even if you don't know the product well. You must believe you are good enough to find the ANSWER when you have no clue. Change your belief to "I'm good enough to represent you, Mr. Customer, and build trust with you." Always do what you say you're going to do regardless of product knowledge and experience. You have to believe you are good enough to master this business one day. (Read my brother Stan Beecham's book, *Elite Minds*.)

2. The longer I am in business, the more I realize how much I don't know. Most rookie salespeople start slow because of a lack of product knowledge. Unfortunately, the way you get more product knowledge is by doing more deals. You can only do more deals by going out and meeting customers. It is a vicious cycle, but if you start with "I don't know" and "I'm going to learn as the situation presents itself" you will go faster, quicker. Believe you can do that as good or better than anybody else.

3. You have got to understand that *people cannot buy from you if they don't know you exist.* Try to think of ways to let people know that you're in this business. A lot of times people remember you for your other business or from how they first met you. You can't shop at the store next door if you don't know what they're selling. People must know that you're open for business, and that typically means you must tell them! (Book: *What's My Buzz?*, from yours truly.)

You must find a way to leave what you do with every person you come in contact with. Even your mother! The easiest way is to ask them what they do or how their business is going. When you do this, they typically will ask you about your business as well. That's when you paint better pictures of what you are looking for.

In the real estate business, you do not want to be a secret agent as the saying goes! You have to get your butt out and see/talk to people who you know!

4. You must do marketing/prospecting, that's "CONSTANT and CONSISTENT" (see chapter on this). You must do the same thing multiple times on a frequent basis. You can put out a newsletter every day or every week. You can make phone calls every day or every week. You can drive to people's offices every day or every week. You can advertise on the Internet or in the local paper every day or every week. It's just like with your finances, you must pay your bills once a month. You've got to do marketing on a consistent basis. So put something into play that you can do on a regular basis to market your business. (See chapter "Creating New Habits.")

Every week, I write an email newsletter. Every week, I get a deal from the newsletter. I schedule time to put out the newsletter and I collect emails from people I meet or from emails I have been sent every day. The main thing is I am consistent in doing this chore and it pays off. Master one piece of marketing and make it a habit before you add another. Each time you add another marketing habit you will dramatically increase your business if you stay consistent.

I believe if you do these three things, you're on the road to getting your referral business kicked off. A good rule of thumb is to spend at least 75 percent of your time prospecting and marketing your first year, 50 percent your second year, and 25 percent every year after. This is the most important activity in building your business.

Hobbies

I was hunting in South Dakota with my friend Trummie, a very successful insurance agent. I asked him why he had not retired yet since he was in his seventies. He told me he had basically been retired for twenty years. I said, "No you haven't."

He said, "Beech, I used to go to work so I could have time to play, but I changed my mindset to go play until the work shows up. When I did that, business picked up and I started having more fun. I go hunting, fishing, or playing with my grandkids, then when the phone rings, I do a deal and then go back to playing." That one conversation changed my mindset on how I do business.

Think about successful insurance agents. A lot of them play golf regularly. They say if you want to play golf every day, get into the insurance business. You get to spend four hours plus, one-on-one, and build a deeper relationship with them. That is a lot more time than a cup of coffee or lunch.

If you take a person fishing at a local lake, you get to spend hours with them. If you go on a motorcycle ride, you usually spend a whole day with them. If you go to a car race with them, you spend a whole day with them. If you take them canoeing or rafting, you get to spend a whole day with them. If you take them on a boat ride on the lake, you get to spend a whole day with them and their family. If you invite them to go to deer camp, you get two to three days with them. If you invite them to the beach for the weekend, you get to spend three days with them.

I think you get my point. Most of us just need ten to twenty good referral sources to drive most of our income. If you spend some hobby/fun time with them, it changes the relationship. It makes it deeper and more personal. You want a personal relationship more than you want a business relationship and inviting people to participate with you in your hobbies is one of the best ways to do that.

Start inviting people you know to go play with you. "Can Johnny come out and play?" Remember that as a kid? Just keep it up in the adult version. Do it often.

Now, look at the hobbies you have and assess if you are doing them with the right people. A lot of folks do it with the same people repeatedly. Are they sending business your way? Maybe you need to ask some other folks to go with you.

My friend Joe asked me if I rode dirt bikes when I was a kid. I told him I did, and he said why don't you get another dirt bike and start riding with us. He had a group of about five to ten people that rode a lot. Every year, they went out west to Colorado and rode. He told me if I wanted to go, I could come along for a local ride and try his bike out, so I did. Next thing I know, I'm buying a dirt bike.

For many years we rode out west and then on one of the trips, I dreamed up the idea we should ride our dirt bikes across the United States so we could tell our grandkids. The next year, we started a trip from Mexico to Canada. After that, we rode from Charleston, South Carolina, to Coos Bay Oregon. Eighty percent of the time on dirt roads and trails. These were dirt bikes, not road bikes or Harleys!

Today as I write this, I still ride often and now I do it on the street. I plan rides that are unique and fun and invite people to go who have motorcycles. I get to spend a whole day riding in the North Georgia mountains with some guys doing what I love and giving them the chance to do what they love.

The key is to put it together and invite people. I make my hobby happen and I make it happen with others and that helps me build deeper friendships.

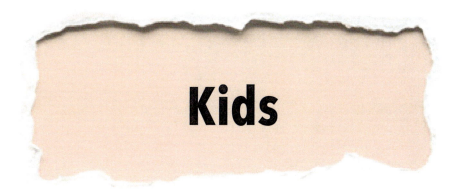

Kids

A lot of us have kids. A lot of us know people that have kids. One of the best ways to grow your businesses is with your kids because it gives you an opportunity to meet lots and lots of new people.

I remember when my kids were small, I would sign up to coach their team. I started noticing I had an opportunity to talk to the parents in a way I wouldn't have if I had been doing something else, like sitting in the stands or just dropping them off.

Usually in Little League, there are ten to twenty kids on the team, depending on if it's basketball, soccer, or football. There is an opportunity at every practice or game for you to pick one of the parents out and have a deeper conversation with them. It's a great opportunity to really get to know somebody in an atmosphere that's not pushy. Most salespeople are always looking for that kind of atmosphere.

Don't be that parent who sits in the stands beside the same person every time and just has a conversation with the person you already know. Use this time to get to know other parents. Be the parent who volunteers to throw the party at the end of the year or helps pick up balls in the outfield. If you volunteer, you can always ask another mom or dad to come help you!

MOM IN THE STANDS—I took my daughter Elyse to her first softball practice. When I arrived, I noticed the coaches were out on the field, so I looked for a place to sit. I noticed a mom sitting at the top of the stands by herself. I walked up the bleachers and sat on the other end of the stands from her. I asked her how she was doing, and she said, "Not good."

"Why?" I asked. "What's wrong?"

The mom began to tell me that her contractor didn't finish her basement remodeling job. He did everything but hang a ceiling fan. The reason was the fan had been put on backorder and just came in today. The remodeler finished her basement last week and could not get by this week to hang the fan. The reason why it was a big deal to her was she had her husband's office party this weekend and she didn't want to have a HOLE in her ceiling.

I then asked her if she wanted the fan hung tonight or tomorrow night.

She looked at me kind of funny and said, "Do you hang ceiling fans?"

I told her I was in the mortgage business and knew a good electrician and that I would call him. My electrician Wes said he'd go over the next day and hang it on his way home from work.

I called Wes several days later and he was so thankful because not only did she pay him handsomely for the fan, but she hired him to do some more work in her basement. The very next day, the mom told her friend about me, and she inquired about a loan to do her basement!

Use this situation with your kids or grandkids as a great opportunity to meet other people. I miss those days at the ball field because I met a lot of parents and grandparents. I think it's one of the most powerful ways to meet new people. It is easy to do because you have something in common.

If you don't have kids, then maybe use your dog. If you walk your dog, don't just walk your dog around your own neighborhood, go to the park and walk. Your dog gives you an opportunity to run into other people that are walking their dogs. In my town, a local entrepreneur is opening a dog park that serves beer and food. The idea is you can meet new folks and there is a sense of community that can be built around your dog.

When you coach a team, you will have deeper conversations with parents. They want to talk to you about their kids' playing time or what they can practice on at home to help their kids get better. You also get everyone's email and phone number. I always put the email addresses in my email newsletter database after the season.

There are many ways to volunteer for your kids' activities. You can coach the team in their favorite sport. You can get involved in their school with PTA, WATCHDOGS, or be a classroom parent. Be a scout leader if they are into that. Just do something as it shows a great example to your kids that you really care about them.

Creating New Habits

We all want to grow our business.

How do we do that?

Create a new prospecting/marketing habit.

You have the same habits every day. When you get up, when you go to bed, and at the office, you have the same habits.

Once you get used to that new habit, then you can add another habit. Every prospecting/marketing habit you add will bring new clients every month! You only need to add one habit, but it must be something you can do all the time. Constantly and consistently every day, week, and month.

When I first started, I began with an email newsletter. I got in the habit of doing the newsletter every month. I scheduled a time to do it on Thursday night after work so it would go out on the first Friday of the month. Nothing could keep me from making sure it went out at the same time every month. It became so successful that I got into the habit of doing it every week. I picked Friday because that's when real estate agents take people out on the weekend. That newsletter now generates four to five deals a month. I've been doing it for years and now my son, who has joined me in the business, does the newsletter. You need a habit like that.

When I first did it, I got people who emailed me and said don't spam me. It hurt my feelings, but I had a pro coaching me and he kept saying, "But five hundred people didn't." Don't worry about the bad apples, just stay focused on getting it out to the people who like it.

I started making it a habit to add people to the newsletter every day. Every new email address I received went into that database.

Every business card I collected went into that database. This was a habit within the first habit. But you have to create the first habit first!

I've already created the habit of sending newsletters, now I'm creating a habit of making videos. I do videos for my mortgage business and videos for my speaking business. The speaking came first. I started walking to work every day to get exercise and came up with the idea of doing inspirational videos while I walked. I did it every day, Monday–Friday, and posted it on Facebook. Then I made it a habit to post it on Instagram and Twitter too. Now it's automatic. I do one almost every morning I walk.

Then I decided I needed a new habit of videos for my mortgage business. Once a month, we hire a young videographer to come to the office and cut about four videos for the month—one to send out every Wednesday. During the month, I listen to what issues my customers are having and that helps me determine what the videos need to be about.

Another habit I have is attending Rotary Club. I go every Friday morning about fifty times a year. I see about one hundred folks there every Friday. Because I have that habit, I get about 1–2 deals a month from the Rotary Club.

You probably already have some habits in place and if you analyze your business, you will see that most of your business comes from those daily habits. Most people have a habit of going to the ball field with their kids, going to church, and maybe something else like PTA or chamber of commerce. The secret is to add a new habit because you have already conquered those.

What about healthy habits? Start a daily workout routine at the gym. You can't believe how many people you can meet at your local gym. Start healthy eating habits by introducing more vegetables and nonfat proteins into your diet.

The idea is for you to block out the time you would for a doctor's appointment and make that prospecting/marketing time slot nonnegotiable. If you do something significant, people will be counting on you.

Here is a small list of new habits you can create:

- Stop by someone's office on the way to or from lunch.
- Add a newsletter by email or snail mail—even if it is the company one.
- Join a local business group: Rotary, Chamber, BNI.
- Go to a small group for a Bible study.
- Show up at PTA and volunteer.
- Take a customer or prospect to dinner with your spouse every week.
- Make videos.
- Post on social media.
- Leave early on Friday after lunch and go visiting.
- Time-block the new habit on your calendar.
- Invite past clients to lunch once a week.
- Host quarterly client appreciation parties.

Create a new habit and stay with it until it becomes a habit, then create another habit. Each habit will generate new business. It is really that simple.

Mayor of Your Village 1

If you want people to call you for business or to refer you to someone, then you should consider being the "Mayor of Your Village."

Being the "Mayor of Your Village," in my mind, is being the "go-to person" for everyone's problems in your town. If you have ever associated with a mayor, all they do is field complaints from citizens. "I need my pothole fixed," "My garbage wasn't picked up last week." The mayor then says, "I will get the road crew right over, I will let the sanitation department know, etc." They just take problems and then solve them for the citizens/voters/customers.

Since we know that if someone has pain, and you can solve that pain, you will be their hero. We also know that businesspeople see one person's pain as their pleasure. If I need to decide which bike to buy, there is another person who sells bikes that would love to talk to me. If you become the middleman and introduce us to each other, you become the hero times two. You get two new people to love you.

Being the "Mayor of Your Village" is all about *connecting people*. Finding out what their pains and pleasures are. When I first thought of this, I was blown away by how easy this made calling people to talk. No more cold calling, just calling people and figuring out what their pains and pleasures were. I now call people I already know every day and ask them if they have a pain I can help with or a pleasure I can tell others about.

To get started being the mayor, you need to build a list of everyone you already know. Get out a piece of paper and start writing down all your family members. My objective is to write down everybody I can in my family. Don't leave anyone out, even if they live far away or you don't like them very much. I can write down my brother, my uncle, and my cousins, etc. I call this the family category. As we go through this, write the names down by category.

As I scroll through all my relationships in life, I start as a youngster and move toward the current month. I start writing down the people I went to high school with (band, sports, nerds), college (fraternity brothers, athletes, and roommates). Then, I think about my first job, my second job, and the people I worked with. Then, think about the customers you had in each of your previous jobs. Next, we list people we know from church, garden club, Rotary, PTA, and our kids' sports. Then, to people we know in business in our community and stay-at-home moms and dads. Don't forget about plumbers, hairdressers, painters, attorneys, etc. You get the idea. Write down everybody who knows your name. That will be a warm call. If they don't know your name, it's a cold call and we only want warm ones.

I'm building a list (a sphere of influence list) and I want to fill a whole page up and then expand on that. These are the people I'm going to start contacting. Some I may call more often, but at least once a year, I'm going to call all these people.

How will the call go? The first thing is to let them know you were thinking about them. Talk about something you did together. Then you'll want to tell them you will be meeting a lot of new people as you prospect for business. And, you want to make sure if you meet someone with a pain, you are clear on what their pleasure is—what their hobby or business expertise is.

Uncle Joe might be a good gunsmith and you might need his knowledge to pass on to someone who is looking to buy a new shotgun for hunting. Let Uncle Joe know you might have to put him on a three-way call someday. Or Aunt Sally might be a real estate agent and you might run into someone looking to buy a home and you want to know what a good or bad lead is for her.

I always want to leave the call with a perfect understanding of how I can leave them with a connection that would be fun and valuable to them. People love this! But another thing usually happens. They usually tell you during the conversation what their pain is. Uncle Joe starts talking about his bad hip and you just happen to know an orthopedic surgeon you can introduce him to. Aunt Sally says she has this house listed with a leaky roof and you just might know a roofer to introduce her to.

Hope you get the point. Make a list and warm call these people as often as you can. Always ask for their pains and pleasures so you can hook them up with someone else.

"Picking up the phone to catch up with a friend may do more for your friendship than sending a simple text. A new study finds that giving people a phone call creates stronger social bonds than sending a text or email. Researchers say an actual call makes people feel more socially 'connected' when it comes to building a relationship with strangers or long-lost friends." [1]

---

[1] StudyFinds. "You Can Talk on Phones, Too: Calling Someone Builds Stronger Social Connection than Texting Them." Study Finds, November 17, 2020. https://studyfinds.org/phone-calls-build-stronger-connections-than-texting/.

Mayor of Your Village 2

Once you've listed everyone you know, and you've got at least one hundred names down, it's time to move to part two. Part two is putting them in some sort of sequence and contact database so you can stay in contact with them on a consistent basis. The most efficient way is to use your cell phone that's synced to your desktop or laptop computer. You want the information to reside in both places. The next thing to do is take all the names you wrote down and call them. Hopefully, you have over 150. Most people know 150 people and divide that by thirty days. We are going to call everyone on the list in the next twenty-five business days to jump-start our referral business.

That's six a day. Next, I want you to take the names and spread them out over the next twenty-five business days until you have six on each day. Now, don't put all your cousins on the first day, spread them out over the month. The objective is to call those six people that day. When do you call them? I leave my house at seven thirty to be at my office by eight o'clock. So, at seven thirty every morning, I have an appointment on my phone to call those six people. My goal is to call all six before the day is out. I just use seven thirty because it lets me know on the way to work who I will be calling. Most of the time I call those people on the way to work if I think they are up.

Put six names in every day and preload those in your phone, Outlook, Gmail, or whatever you use. Now, you've got all 150 names to call them in the next thirty days. You've never called that many people, especially people you already know. I bet you $100, if you call all of those people in the next thirty days, you will double your business.

A lot of times, I'll call people and say, "I was just thinking about you, how you doing today?"

Each morning, I'll look at a name. Say it's Greg Bennett. That day, I say to myself, *I need to call Greg today.* So, I call Greg. "Greg, this is Beech. How you doing? How's the video business. How's your wife, how're the kids, blah, blah, blah." And we talk about *Greg*. We *don't* talk about Steve. I want to know as much about what's going on with him, because Greg is my friend and I care and want Greg to be successful. And, I want him to do well. I'm just letting him know that, hey, I'm thinking about you. After I talk to Greg, I decide when I want to talk to Greg again. I may want to talk to him next week.

Next month, next year, it doesn't matter. It's a matter of what feels comfortable to you. For real estate agents or people who are hiring me to speak, I may talk to them once a week or every two or three weeks. I'm going to talk to them fairly frequently. But a fraternity brother or an old neighbor—I might only talk to them every six months. But after I spoke to Greg, I'm going to move him to when I *want* to talk to him again. I'll put him on that date at seven thirty a.m., three to six months from now.

The secret is you can forget about him for now. And then, when that day comes, it'll pop up on your calendar. So, call people and then move them to a future date so it will pop up and remind you to call them again.

If I get to the office that morning and I see Greg's name in my calendar, and I think, *I'm not really in the mood to talk to him today*, I don't force myself to call him. I just move him to another day. I might move him off until the next day or, I may move him off to next week or next month. It doesn't matter. Once he's in my phone, he's going to stay in my phone as a contact. So, take the names, and input them into your calendar at the same time every time.

My marketing plan for every day is to try to contact six people. Now, here's the cool part. If you put it in your phone and it syncs with your desktop, you can check your phone while on the road to call people instead of listening to the radio. You can call one on the way to work, when you get to work, or when you get a free moment. You can look up someone else on your list on your computer and call another one. Then, if you've got to meet somebody for lunch, you get in your car and you call another. I hardly ever listened to the radio in the car. I'm always talking on the phone to one of my warm contacts, somebody in my village.

At the office when I'm caught up on stuff, I look at my calendar, figuring out who I need to call, and I call them. Sometimes I call that day. Some days I don't get to call any of them, and I move them off and catch them next week. You have to get in the habit of doing something consistently in your marketing. I have found this is the easiest way to market your business because you're not calling them to ask them to send you a customer. And you're only calling people who know you. So, there's no cold calling.

This is just staying in touch with the people who already know about you. An amazing thing happens when you start calling those people. Most of them (I have found about 75 percent of them) realize our calls have been all about them, and they'll turn around and ask, "Beech, how's the speaking business, how's the mortgage business?" And that's when I get to tell them about my business only because they asked. I'm not putting anything in front of them they didn't ask for. Make a list right now and put as many names as you can in your phone or in your Outlook or whatever you use. Put in as many names as you can so you can start the process of calling those people when you've got a free minute.

Mayor of Your Village 3

You've written down everyone you know in your village or your sphere of influence. You've taken all those names and you've put them on a calendar on your phone or your desktop so you know when to call them.

Now, the next thing you have to think about is when they do ask how your business is, you have to be able to respond. If you've been to my workshop, we call that your perfect customer. You need to ask yourself who is your perfect client. Who am I looking for? If my uncle asked me, "How's business?"

I can say, "Hey, business is great," but he doesn't know how to help me with that. I've got to tell him something to give him the opportunity to refer me.

So, I "Paint Better Pictures" (see future chapter). I need to give him pictures of things to look for or pictures that may show up in his day-to-day activities. When he sees those pictures he says, "Oh yeah, I need to call Steve. I need to tell Steve about that." Or, "I need to tell this person about Steve."

What are a couple of different pictures that I could paint for people that allow them to know who or what I'm looking for? In the mortgage business, we have five customers. We have the first-time home buyer, the second-time home buyer, the move-up home buyer, the move-down home buyer, and someone buying an investment property or a second home. So, depending on who I'm talking to, I'm going to paint them a picture of one of those five people if I want them to send me mortgage referrals.

In the speaking business, I may come up with some ideas of some companies and some individuals I need to meet. I ask questions like "Do you know anyone at Coke?" Coke is a picture.

Then if he or she says yes, I want to get in contact with that person and ask the Coke employee if they know any regional sales managers. The regional manager could hire me to speak. But, if I ask my uncle if he knows a regional sales manager, he doesn't see that as a picture so he probably won't give me a referral.

"My speaking business is great, but you don't happen to know anyone at Citibank do you? I'm really trying to meet somebody there to see if I can train their salespeople." Or I'll ask, "Do you know anyone at State Farm or Travelers Insurance?"

He responds, "I don't, Steve, why?"

I say, "Well, they all have salespeople. And you know, what I do is I go in and train their salespeople how to be better at getting referral business."

And he might say, "You know, I don't really know Travelers, but how about AAA insurance? I got a buddy of mine in my Sunday school class who works at AAA."

I say, "Yeah, I'd love to meet him." So that's a picture my uncle understood. I've got to know how to lay that out for him, in the world he lives and works in.

If I'm with my son and he comes home with one of his friends, they're usually like twenty-three to twenty-five years old. They will ask, "How's the mortgage business, Mr. Beecham?"

I respond, "Great. You guys know, a lot of your friends are getting married and when they get married, they want to buy a house. So next time you go to a wedding, I want you to make sure, if they're going to be buying a house, don't forget to tell them about me." So that's a picture that they're going to see.

Think about who your perfect customers are and how you can explain to a complete stranger what it is you're looking for without going into all of that stuff like your unique selling proposition. Just look at the person in front of you and figure out a way you can get customers from them.

Another picture to paint is which companies in your town you would really like to have a relationship with. Or, if you could meet them today, who are five people who could possibly change your life? And, what I find is that most people in their town don't know exactly who they want to meet. In other words, there may be a plant in your town and you're a financial advisor or a real estate agent. You'd really like to meet the HR person at that plant, but you've never really gone and done the research to find out who that person is. All you have to do is Google them and go on their webpage. That's John Smith, head of HR at ABC manufacturing. So, what you should want to do when people ask, "How's your real estate business?" is say, "It's great. You know, I'm really trying to meet John Smith at ABC manufacturing. You don't, by any chance know him?" And that's the way you want to present it to people, because then the people around you can help you because it's clear to them what it is you're looking for. You have to remember that other people don't think like you think, they're thinking about what's going on in *their* world, not what's going on in *your* world. It's your job to bring them into your world, to give them the picture so they can think about you.

WRITE DOWN THE NAMES.
PUT THEM IN YOUR PHONE CALENDAR ON A CERTAIN DAY TO CALL.
FIND THEIR PAIN AND PLEASURE.
WHEN THEY ASK, PAINT THEM A PICTURE OF WHO YOU WANT TO MEET.

A-List

Most of us have had some sales training. When you do, they teach about an A, B, C list of customers and prospects. The A-list is the best who make you the most money. The C-list is the lower end and you might drop them from any list if they don't buy in a short period of time.

The question is, do you have an A-list of customers? [1] Depending on your business, it is probably ten to fifty people maximum. These people account for or could account for 80 percent of your business. I think you should maintain two types of A-list customers. One is for the top customers you have now and you want to stay in touch with so you don't lose that business. They are not only customers, but you should be looking to make them your friends. Then there is the A-list of prospects. These are the people who if you could get their business, they could change your life. They are probably already on someone else's A-list but, you want to stay in touch with them in case the other person disappoints them and you can pick up their business. [2]

A-list customers and prospects need to hear from you on a weekly to biweekly basis. These are also the same people you buy presents for at Christmas and T-shirts when you are out of town and you see something they would like. Treat these folks like they are your family because they are. They also need to see you

---

[1] Stark, Karl, and Bill Stewart. "Who Are Your A-List Customers? | Inc.Com." Inc. Accessed September 26, 2023. https://www.inc.com/karl-and-bill/who-are-your-a-list-customers.html.

[2] Dan. "Do You Know Who Your A-List Customers Are?" The Strategic CFO®, March 4, 2008. https://strategiccfo.com/articles/profitability/do-you-know-who-your-a-list-customers-are/.

socially. Take them to lunch, dinner, or a Braves game. Buy them concert tickets or books on their favorite hobbies.

The B-list is the customer or prospect that is doing a little business with you but you probably don't have all their business. You might not be the first person they call but they keep you in the game. You want to stay in touch with your B-list customers bi-weekly to monthly.

C-list are those customers you are looking to fire and replace with A-list customers. They send you business rarely and when they do, they are a pain in the ass. C-list prospects are ones that call when their normal guy can't get the job done. Your C-list prospects are the ones you may have done business with in the past, but they have another person who gets most of their business and you are holding on until you can replace them or get them back on board.

In my world of real estate agents and people who hire me to speak, we have a lot of C-list clients and prospects. You don't want to drop them because at any moment they could become an A-lister. This has happened to me a lot in the last thirty years, so I stay in contact with them every month to six months.

How do you keep up and organize these lists of prospects? Use a good CRM system and ensure you time-block on your calendar when the calls will take place.

Constant and Consistent Advertising

A long time ago when I had my clothing store, I used to advertise infrequently in the local newspaper. I always thought my results were bad. One day, I asked the advertising guy what I could do to make my ads work. He told me to copy what the shoe industry does.

There was a women's shoe store in town and the owner ran the smallest ad he could every week, always in the same place. And though it was small, people noticed it every week. The ad just had a picture of a lady's shoe and the name, phone number, and address of the store. That was it. No discount or anything. I visited the owner of the shoe store and he told me, "You need to be constant in your ads. Constantly running and consistent by doing the same ad."

Later I read Peter Glen of Vermont's marketing book and he said the same thing. When I got into the mortgage business, I tried to think of something I could be constant and consistent with, and at that time, email was starting to become *the thing*. I hired a friend of mine, and we came up with an email newsletter—but we made it about the community, not about mortgages. I have been doing that for twenty-five years. I send it out every week religiously.

Then I added calling people to my marketing plan. I always call people every day and I developed a system to remind me who and when to call each person. I do it constantly and consistently.

Do not be sporadic in your marketing. Try a few different things, but if something is working make it constant and consistent. They work.

My first business was a clothing store. We spent a lot of money on marketing to the local community. One of the most effective pieces we did was a letter. I wrote a letter to people who lived within a small radius of my store but also lived in the nicer neighborhoods. I was selling expensive stuff, so I needed to hit the people who had money. The letter was just addressed to the postal route and not to the individual who lived there because I didn't have their names. In the letter, I talked about my store and the types of clothing we sold which were traditional men's and ladies'. Think suits, not sportwear. I mentioned the brands and the custom-fitting service we offered. Long story short, it was successful, so we did it every year.

Then, years later when I was in the mortgage business, the interest rates dropped a full point one day because of the economy going into a recession so I decided to send a similar letter. The letter simply said rates had dropped and if you were looking for someone local to refinance your house and save money, I would like to help. BAM! That was a huge success. Next thing I knew, every one of the loan officers in my company wanted the letter. Still, to this day, there are folks who do that when the rates drop. They not only mail to their customer base but they pull up data at the courthouse and sort through who would have a higher rate and would be interested in saving money.

I bring this up because one thing that works in one business can work in another business. Every time rates decrease I pull out this letter and mail it.

Go Deep

As I started really focusing on why people refer you more business, I discovered it was all about the relationship. It's about having a deeper relationship. I want to talk to you about what I call Going Deep. I think we fail to go *deep* when we are with other people. Because we don't go deep with them, our relationships remain on the surface.

So how do we go deeper? I want you to think of yourself as a reporter who's writing an article on the person in front of you. Act like you are writing for the local newspaper and you are interested in everything about this person. You want to know how they got started. You want to know about their family life, their successes and failures. I want you to really concentrate when you're talking to somebody. When we are in a conversation with another person, your natural tendency is to say, oh I did that or yeah, I know him or I used to be in that business. Understand they don't really care about that. Yes, you heard that right. They don't care about you or what you know or where you have been or what you have done. They only want to talk about themselves and want you to hear their story.

What you want to do is focus on going deep with this person. As deep as you can. You want to know as much about them as they're willing to tell you. I call it going down the veins of their life. Big mountains have veins that go deep, and each vein is different. So, the veins I use when talking with others are things like family, business, and hobbies. Each of these is a vein and I want to go as deep in each vein as they will let me. The more they will tell me, the more I know about what makes them tick.

When you go down these veins, an amazing thing happens.

Seventy-five percent of them will notice the whole conversation has been about them. They will then say, "Tell me about you, what do you do for a living? What is your family like? What do you do for fun?" When they ask you what you do for a living then, *paint them a picture* of what you are looking for.

One day, my wife called me and told me Jeff Foxworthy was speaking at my kid's school assembly. He was a founder of the private school and so he was invited to speak to the kids. I got to the school late and ran into Jeff in the parking lot as he was leaving the school. He asked me, "Do you have kids in school, what are their names, what grades, do they like the school?"

I told him they loved the school and their stupid uniforms. He said, "You sound like you're from around here." I told him I was from Roswell. He then asked me if I knew his first wife, Nancy, who was in my homeroom. After that short conversation, I could not get over how great I felt because he made the whole conversation about me. He dug deep into me and never talked about his celebrity status.

So, think about going deeper with people, not just surface social conversation. A typical conversation may go like this: "How are you doing?"

"I'm doing fine. How are you doing?"

"I'm doing fine. What did you do this weekend?"

"We went to a kid's soccer game. What did you do this weekend?"

"We went to the mountains and hiked."

Try to change your way of conversing. When you ask them a question, don't give your answer. I find when we ask someone a question, we don't really care or listen to their answer. What we typically do is spend time, while they are answering us, coming up with our own answer.

Learn to forget about you! Just go deep with them, and learn as much about them as you can. It builds trust quicker because they think you care about them, and you do need to care about them. Trust is the first ingredient you need with someone to get them to spend money with you or promote you. The deeper you go with them, the more trust you develop.

Always remember to look them in their *left eye*! As you are facing them, it is *their* left eye, not the eye to your left which is their right eye. Psychologists say that looking someone in their left eye makes it a more heartfelt conversation. If you look them in the right eye, that means you're trying to do business with them and you're getting serious about numbers and stuff. So, look them in the left eye.

Go as deep as you can next time you are in a conversation with a stranger or a family member. Look them in their left eye and see how long it takes for them to realize they need to ask you questions.

WHEN THEY DO, PAINT THE PICTURE OF WHAT YOU ARE LOOKING FOR!
BAM!

I took my youngest son, Colin, to the Masters Tournament. That night after the tournament was over, my wife, Mary, and the two older kids called and said, "We want you to try out for *The Apprentice*. They are having tryouts tomorrow and we think you would be good at it." So, the next morning we went to the tryouts along with three hundred other people.

As I was waiting for my turn, Colin said, "Use your book on them, Dad." I sent Colin to see where everybody was going. When my time came to interview, I told him to sit on the sofa and watch me work my book.

I decided to meet the other ten candidates that were interviewing with me. The first guy was a book publisher. I told him I had published a book. The next guy was a commercial real estate guy, and we talked about real estate since I had some commercial properties. The next one was a fireman from Rattlesnake Ridge, where I had done some volunteer work, and the last one was a cheerleader from The University of Tennessee. I mentioned I met my wife, who was my cheerleading partner. Then, we were called into a room for the interview. The lady in charge asked everybody in the room who they would vote for to be the next apprentice. All the candidates I met in the lobby said they would choose me. She called me afterward and said, "You're the first guy who ever had that many people vote for them."

I went back for the second interview. When I sat down, she asked, "How did you lose your job?"

"I didn't lose my job," I said.

She said, "Well, this next *Apprentice* is only for those who lost their jobs."

I then told her that my wife didn't tell me that part! So, I didn't get to be on *The Apprentice* but, by spending less than fifteen seconds, I got someone to vote for me. They picked me because I made the conversation about them.

Direct Connect

This is a powerful, not often-used marketing idea.

If you believe *giving* referrals will increase the number of referrals you receive, then this will turbo-charge your referrals.

Next time someone asks you for a referral, and you have one for them, put them on hold and call the referral source you want to connect them to. When the referral source answers, then make it a three-way call and directly connect the two. "Jim, this is Wes, my electrician. Wes, this is Jim, my friend. His wife just bought a chandelier and needs it hung this week because they are having a big party."

If you call the referral source and you get their voicemail, then still make it a three-way call and leave a message. "Wes, this is Beech, I have my friend Jim on the line. Say hi, Jim. Jim needs a chandelier hung this week. Jim, leave your cell number for Wes." Then he does, and I say, "Wes, please give him a call and I will send each of you the other's contact info."

When you do this, you create a "WOW" for each person. When you give someone a WOW, they want to reciprocate. Maybe they will send you a customer.

Most of us don't do this because of the time it takes to do it. But I promise it is time well spent. It gives you the opportunity to brag about the other guys. But, most importantly, it makes sure they know you *gave them the referral.* A lot of times someone asks for a referral, and you give them one, then you run into the referral person and ask them if Jim called, and they say no never heard from him. This eliminates that. When you directly connect, you are sure the other person knows you sent a referral. Also, this way you know they will get a call back. If someone gives you a lead, you probably won't call them. But if a lead calls you and asks you to call them back, then you are for sure going to call.

When you connect somebody on the spot by putting them both on the phone, you create a WOW with them, and then reciprocity kicks in, and you get twice the referrals you would ordinarily get!

If you have a lot of past clients, always offer to help them with a referral to one of your vendors. Use this process to impress them, to WOW them.

After I taught Mark about "Direct Connect," he had a past client call him who needed a contractor to finish his garage apartment. So, he used "Direct Connect." He called one of his contractors and his past client on a three-way call. Both were happy with the situation and with Mark for hooking them up with each other.

Hang Out Where the Money Is

I heard a guy say one day that if you want to do home loans in the country club, then you need to join that country club. A better statement has never been made!

You get business from the places you spend the most time.

If you are hanging out with losers, you will get losers calling for business. However, if you hang out with rich people, you will get rich people calling you. Start asking people you know who are in the service business where all their business comes from. They will tell you from their church, neighborhood, or golf club. It's where they spend a lot of time. They probably are very active in it too.

If you want to get more business, start hanging out where your potential customers are.

If you are a real estate agent, hang out at the HOA and PTA meetings.

If you are a financial advisor, hang out at collector car shows and golf courses.

If you are a banker, join the chamber of commerce and Rotary Clubs.

If you are a divorce attorney, go to the bars where the recently separated go or to a gym. My wife, Mary, and I joke every time we see someone getting back into shape, they are about to get divorced.

If you want to get into the luxury market of your chosen field, pay for a golf club membership. Carve out time to play golf with different groups every week. You won't believe how many referrals you will receive from their network.

You might want to join a pickleball club as this is now a popular sport among older affluent adults.

Now don't just hang out at one spot, go to multiple spots. The more hangouts you do, the more business you will get. I can't spend money with you if I don't know you exist!

Hang out where your people are!

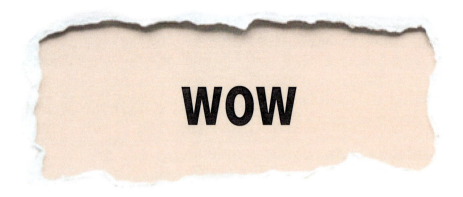

How do you create a "WOW" with others?

By giving more than what is asked.

We all think we have great customer service, but we all complain about each other's customer service. The secret is to WOW your customers.

If I provide a service to you and it is what you expected, then you don't necessarily tell anyone because you got what you paid for. However, if I give you *more* than you expected, it creates a WOW, and then you go tell others. The opposite is true if you do *less* than I expected. I will tell everyone how terrible you are. So always do more than expected, and people will talk about you.

Let's say I run into my friend downtown, and I ask them how things are going. She says everything is good, but Little Johnny is really struggling in English and she has to spend time with him every day tutoring him. I would tell her about my friend Terri, who has a tutoring business, or I'd tell her about my friend Cookie, who was a teacher for thirty years and does tutoring on the side. I would gauge her response and then connect her to one of them. She leaves and goes, WOW. That was nice of Steve to do that." The other side is that now one of my friends will get a call and also say, WOW. That was nice of Steve to think of me." Two WOWs at one time!

If I am doing a loan for you, I will have a deeper conversation about the new house. I want to know what things you plan on doing immediately when you move in. If you say paint and change out some light fixtures, I will ask if you have a painter and electrician. If you need one, I'll get my friend on the phone—with you—right away, introduce you to them, and ask my contractor buddy to help you out. I have two more WOWs!

If I am at a networking event and meet you, I will ask you who your favorite customer is. I'll get you to paint me a better picture of who you want to meet. Then, I will start asking if you would like to meet certain people. Hopefully one of my friends is a good contact for you. If so, I get two more WOWs!

Always try to help people by offering your contacts to them. This simple, daily activity gets me a lot of business because you are referring people out to others and both of them feel they need to reciprocate and send you a referral.

Add tasks to your process checklists that include ways to give your clients something they did not expect. Something that goes above and beyond what others in your field are doing. They will remember these simple acts of doing more than expected. For example, delivering pizza to clients on their moving day so they don't have to worry about buying lunch. Have their hobbies on your checklist so if you are out and about and you see something that may interest them, you can purchase it for them.

Have a business philosophy of UNDER PROMISE AND OVER DELIVER. People will remember you!

You Are the Average of Your Five Best Friends

I want you to think about where you are in life, where you are socially, where you are economically, and where you are financially. I want you to think about who you hang out with.

What you'll find out is that you're the average of the five closest people to you. One of the ways you can be worse is hanging out with people who are not doing so well financially, they're depressed, or not fun. And the same goes for getting better. If you want to get better, one of the best things you can do is find some better people to hang out with, people who are doing things you're not doing. People who can pull you up instead of push you down. I've told my kids this for years—who you hang with is who you become.

If you are in perfect balance, then you have two friends who you are pulling up. You are mentoring them. You are helping them get better mentally and financially. You are helping them because you have been there and understand where they are. You should also have a friend that's on par with you. Basically, they are going through life at the same speed as you. They are close to you, financially and socially. They are eager to learn and grow from others like you, and they can be the person you compare yourself to, to make sure you are not lagging behind. Then you have two friends who are rock stars in your eyes. They have more money or a better family life. They take more risk and have already been where you are. They coach you up and tell you to not be afraid to step out of line or to try new stuff.

All of these friends are not perfect in every way. They just might be who you coach up financially, but not emotionally. The same for the ones pulling you up. One might be successful financially but not a good family person and the other pulling you up might be the opposite. You have these friends for certain pieces of your life, not necessarily your whole life.

If you're running with a good group of people, then you're going to be a better person. If you're running with people who are getting in trouble and not doing the right things, chances are pretty good you're going to do that too. Your environment is everything. Think about who you're hanging out with.

Am I hanging out with people who can move me up?

That doesn't mean that you need to get rid of your friends who aren't doing as well as you, because there's a place in your life for pulling people up. But some people need to pull you too. So, you have to make sure you've got some people in your group pulling you up and introducing you to new ways to think and new ideas, new ways to look at your business and work-life balance. It'll help you really grow your business if you try to find some friends who can pull you up and make you better.

So how do you find these friends? For pulling you up, seek out what we call mentors. Mentors are folks who are successful in an area you want to grow in. Ask them if you can buy them lunch occasionally. I have five or six of these folks and each one brings a different perspective to the table.

You also need to search out folks you can pull up. That's easy to find if you just look around. Don't wait on them to ask you for help. Offer to help someone in your areas of expertise. You can mentor a new businessperson or a newly married person. If you look hard, you can see the stress in their eyes and just offering them a word of encouragement and asking how they're doing can help wonders. Most of the time they will spill their guts to you if you are good at asking questions first.

PS: Avoid doing this with your adult kids. I try to get my kids to talk to others we know who I think they will listen to and give them good advice.

Remember: You're the average of your five best friends.

Personal Not Professional

Make every interaction personable, not professional.
That way, the customer is doing business with you as a friend and not because your price is low.

My friend Ted owns a restaurant in my town. The food lately has not been up to par and the service has been slow. I'm sure he is having issues with help. But guess what? I keep going back because I have a personal relationship with Ted and he is my friend. If he wasn't my friend, I would have told everybody it wasn't a good spot. But instead, I tell everybody, "It is a great spot, but he is cognizant of the fact he is really struggling with help right now. The service and the food are not up to par, but we should support him because he is a great guy."

Now, I don't know about you, but I'm pretty sure my service is not always excellent. I don't want my good customers not coming back because they had one bad experience. You don't either. So, the way to fix that is to make your relationship more personable than professional.

You start by getting to know your customers better. Don't just ask professional questions about their sales and how the business is doing, start by learning more about their family and what their kids are into. Know more about their spouse and what they do. Discover where they grew up and where they went to school. Ask them questions about how they get business. What kind of marketing do they do? Where do they want to get more business from?

Then, every time you call on them, talk about family and other personal stuff. Invite them to go with you and your spouse to fun things like baseball games. You want to build more of a personal relationship than a professional one. A lot of people do business with folks they like regardless of the cost or delivery time. They want to support their friends. Be that person they want because you are their friend.

The professional side will come and will be talked about at the appropriate time. Friends do business with friends, and they don't quit their friends very easily. You've got to really mess up for your friend to go elsewhere.

They won't avoid your calls if you are calling for personal reasons versus professional reasons. And they'll almost always ask you about your business.

Bring Your Assets, Not Your Agenda

If you went outside and there was a homeless man sitting on the steps, could he help you? NO! He cannot help you with your *agenda*, but we can help him with our *assets*. All we can do is offer him a ride, shower, or food. And because we can only help him with our *assets*, we are not afraid to talk to him because we are not talking about our *agenda*.

Several years ago, I was talking with my friend Kevin Bryant. Kevin has a long history in the sports marketing world. He brought it to my attention that all companies were trying to find a way to get their customers under the water tower. "The water tower" is the saying for meeting people where they are. This is different than hoping they see your ad on TV. It means being in front of people as they go through their day. Do they see you on the way to the grocery store or work? Businesses want you to think of them in your daily travels.

I mentioned that cities didn't realize they had lots of assets: they own parks where people can advertise; things like sponsoring the concession stand or a naming opportunity on a ball field (think about the naming of pro stadiums); they have fire and police vehicles that could be logo'd up like in NASCAR; or street signs and city buildings that could be advertising venues.

This got me thinking that we all have assets, mainly the people we know and the knowledge we have. But are we using our assets to help others? Most of us are *not* doing that. Like we can help a homeless guy with our assets, we can help our neighbors and our customers with our assets.

The main reason we don't cold call people is because we go in with OUR agenda, not theirs. We go in to tell them about how great our product or service is. Then we think they probably don't want to buy our stuff because they already have an insurance guy or a real estate agent. So, we don't approach them. We talk ourselves out of a cold call.

But if you change your mindset and go in with your assets and not YOUR agenda, then they can't hurt your feelings or tell you no. You didn't ask them for anything, you only gave your assets. You asked them how you could help them by introducing them to people. You asked what you could do to help them get more business.

Go in with your assets, not your agenda, and you will always win the person over.

As my friend Dan Merkle asks, would you rather be the one walking down the street hustling others by asking them if they would give you twenty dollars or would you rather be the one walking down the street handing out the twenty dollars to those in need?

How can you help someone today with your assets?

What assets do you have to help someone in your community grow their business?

- Contacts in my phone and/or database
- High school friends
- College friends
- Current and old neighbors
- Knowledge I have from places I worked
- Places and/or people where I have lived or visited

Cloud Referrals

I was speaking to a bunch of financial advisors and one of them mentioned he sent a lot of business to an estate attorney, yet the attorney never sent him any referrals. I suggested he get a new attorney. The problem was this attorney was the only show in town. I asked him if there were other attorneys that did the same thing in the surrounding areas and the answer was yes.

I then told them an idea I developed with real estate agents. I knew I needed several real estate agents to have a successful mortgage business. But I wanted to send them referrals too. I needed twenty or thirty agents and so I wondered how I could send them all business. I came up with the idea I call "Cloud Referrals."

When I had my clothing business, I hired a consultant. He asked me where people went to shop if they couldn't find what they wanted in my store. I told him most people went to the mall where there were more options. He asked me if there were other small men's clothing stores like mine in the metro area. I said there were several. He asked what would happen if I reached out to them and cut a deal with them. The deal is if I don't have what my customer needs and you do have what they need, then I send him to you or I can buy your item at a discounted price. Then, offer to reciprocate with them. If they missed a sale, and I had the item, I would sell it to their customer and not steal the customer or they could come to my store, and I would sell it to them at a discount so they could make some money. What happened was they all started calling me and I would call whichever one I needed. My business increased 20 percent just from the sales to my friendly competitors.

So, do the same thing. Take the town you live in and divide it

A FEW BIG IDEAS   55

up in as many categories as you can. For me, that would be customers looking for golf course communities, condos, townhomes, mini-farms, estate property, divorced groups, first-time home buyers, etc. Then, I pick a real estate agent for each category. That way I can work with five to ten agents in my town. Then, I do the same thing for the neighboring towns. That way, I can send referrals that are in that agent's sweet spots to twenty to thirty agents all year long.

I had the financial advisor think about that and he found out he could refer five different attorneys around his business and not have to give it all to the guy who didn't send him any business. Then, if one attorney was sending him referrals, maybe he'd send him more business. Just because the attorney didn't live in his town didn't mean he couldn't travel to the customer or do a good job.

If you are a real estate agent, you need referrals from painters and remodeling contractors. Look around you and figure out which one you need to refer based on where they live and what they charge. Don't just give out your business to one painter.

Real estate agents can also refer business to other agents in different parts of town where they do not operate. If Mark works the north side of Atlanta, it is very difficult for him to show property south of I-20. So, he has a couple of agents who live on the south side of Atlanta he can call to help service the client. When they have someone looking on the north side of town, guess who they are going to call?

Community Organizations

I asked my friend Lisa to tell me her number one marketing tip. She said being involved in the community has been the best thing for her business. Lisa is a residential real estate closing attorney who also does business contracts and closings.

She said it gives you name recognition! When you get referred by someone, the other person may know of you, which is social credit, which becomes business credit. In other words, the more people know you, the better. If you are involved in the community, you will meet a ton of like-minded, solid people and you will probably end up in the local paper. Lisa has done a good job of not only getting involved in the chamber and the Rotary Club, but she has done a lot of hard work by being on the boards and being in a leadership role. A lot of people now know her name. So, when someone says, "Call Lisa," many times they say they have heard of her. This makes the referral and the trust factors go way up.

There are so many things to get involved with, it can take a lot of your time. But every one of these community organizations you join will probably increase your business by 50 percent. That's right.

When you join most community organizations, you will get in the habit of meeting with that group on a frequent basis, which builds relationships faster.

Good relationships turn into trusting relationships which create more referral business.

What are some things I can get involved with in my community?

Here is a small sampling of places most communities have:

- Chamber of Commerce
- Rotary
- Lions/Kiwanis
- Toast Masters
- Church
- Garden Club
- Historical Society
- Symphony/Theater
- Senior Services
- American Legion
- Youth Sports (coaching, umpire, board)
- Fellowship of Christian Athletes
- Habitat for Humanity
- Homelessness
- Drug/Alcohol Recovery Programs
- Police/Fire
- Food Bank
- Community College
- Parks and Recreation
- Rural Health/Hospitals
- Recycling
- Disabled Adults and Children's Organizations
- Animal Rescue
- Scouting

Michael started a new job as an insurance agent. His boss called me and asked if I would help him get to know some folks. The first thing I did was invite him to my Rotary Club. He became an active member and, because of that, he became very successful. You can do that for a new person in your community or a friend who needs to meet more people.

Events

All your customers and friends want to meet new, exciting people. If you become the conduit for that, then you get more referrals. When people meet new, fun people, they will call you and tell you how much they appreciate it. They will want to reciprocate by introducing you to people you want to meet. [1]

You could start with charity events. There's typically no shortage of charities in your community. Host an event or fundraiser for them. You could have something small like a dinner or do something more elaborate. [2]

I had a close friend whose son needed a heart transplant. Mary and I cooked up the idea we would invite a lot of our friends to a resort about one hour away and have a spend-the-night black-tie event. About twenty couples came and we had our friend stand up and talk about the cost and struggles they were having. I then asked the group to help with donating money and time for their son. Everybody gave some money, and everybody had a great date night weekend while all the ladies got to dress up. It was fun!

I hosted a yard party for another charity. They have an orphanage in Africa, and they needed a place to have the party. They invited a lot of people. I also invited a lot of people from my database. We raised a little money, and I got the chance to meet some of their donors. Donors usually buy big houses! I provided the location and they paid for the food.

---

1 Frederik Nielsen, "10 Community Event Ideas Your Neighbourhood Will Love," Billetto Blog, March 4, 2019, https://billetto.co.uk/blog/community-event-ideas-examples/.
2 Social Tables, "15 Community Event Ideas That Bring People Together," Social Tables, June 22, 2022, https://www.socialtables.com/blog/event-planning/community-event-ideas/.

Some examples:

- Concerts
- Brainstorming sessions
- Agricultural Extension Agent
- Chef dinners
- Events you plan that give you a reason to invite others
- Host a "pie giveaway" at Thanksgiving for your top fifty clients
- Rent a theater for a free movie for your clients and their families
- Host an open house at your office and provide a catered lunch
- Client Appreciation Parties at a local bar/restaurant [3]

---

[3] Sara Elliott, "10 Community Event Ideas," HowStuffWorks, January 25, 2012, https://lifestyle.howstuffworks.com/event-planning/10-community-event-ideas.htm.

Paint Better Pictures

One reason we do not get a lot of referral business is because we fail to paint others a better picture of what we are looking for. Let me say that again.

One reason we do not get a lot of referral business is because we fail to paint others a better picture of what we are looking for.

When you ask someone what they do and are still not clear after they explain it, you tend to ask them more questions. Probe into what it is, exactly, they do.

But what if you asked them to paint you a picture of it? If they did, you would have a clear answer.

If you don't know how to help them with a referral, then, get them to paint a picture of what a great referral would look like for them. An example would be, you are talking to a doctor, and you ask a deeper question of what kind of doctor. They tell you they are an orthopedist. You then ask if they specialize in any type of orthopedic work, and they say they do Tommy John surgeries. Then you ask who you should tell about him and his business. They say, "High school baseball players are my best customers. A kid is pitching in high school and hurts his arm, he needs to see me so we can figure out what to do next." Now you have this visual picture of a kid throwing off the mound at the local high school baseball game. Several days later, you run into your friend at the grocery store, and they have their son with them. You start small talk and find out the kid is on the baseball team at the local high school. Now you can mention to them that if someone hurts their throwing arm, you know the guy they need to see.

Back to the doctor. I find that 75 percent of the time, if I get them to paint me a picture of who they want to meet, they will ask me what I do. That's when *you* paint *them* a picture of who *you* want to meet.

"I'm in the mortgage business, Doc. I love meeting great real estate agents. Ones who work for HomeSouth Residential, Inc., Compass, or Sotheby's. Who's your favorite real estate agent?" Then, "Oh yeah, I don't know her. Could you introduce me to her?"

Or, "Doc, I'm in the speaking business. Do you ever go to any doctor conferences or meetings? Those are the people who usually have me present. I have written several books on growing your business locally, like you getting to the high school coaches and parents, and could help some of the docs out with growing their practices."

Always leave a conversation by painting a picture to someone else of who you are looking to meet. Coke is a picture and soft drink is not. Delta is a picture and airline is not. You get the picture! Give them something about you their brain has never thought of before. Picture-like stories give them a new way to remember you. The more specific the picture, the better the referral will be.

PAINTING MY OWN MOM A BETTER PICTURE—I went to Mom's house and she wondered why I stopped by on a Wednesday at two p.m. I said, "To tell you your grandkids are not going to have Christmas this year."

"Why?" she said.

I replied, "Because I have no customers. How do you think I get my customers?"

"People know you, I guess," she said.

I replied, "You have never referred me a customer, Mom!"

"Didn't know you needed me to," she said.

So, I had to paint a picture for her. "When you go out to eat and the lady says we are buying a mountain house or a beach house, I want to know. When your friends come up to you and have the real estate badge on and it says 'Keller Williams' or 'ReMax,' I want to meet them. Why? Because they send me loans, I get money, and then I buy bicycles for the kids at the local bike shop. Then Santa brings them down the chimney." My mom then knew why I needed her to be on the lookout for people who were buying a new home or for a real estate agent. So, paint a picture of what you want them to send you when they see it.

I painted Cindy Bowers a better picture. I was trying to figure out how I could get more speaking gigs with real estate agents. I could come to sales meetings, do sales training, coaching, etc. I painted this whole picture of how I could help agents with my knowledge of the industry and with my background as an entrepreneur. How agents were basically entrepreneurs.

Well, about two years later, she called and said they were making a sales training change at her company and she had a meeting scheduled for me and the lady who owned the company. I met with her and told her how her agents were entrepreneurs and she went, "WOW, you are right." She then hired me to do a video training series. Paint better pictures!

TO DO: Paint me a picture of who you are looking for and send it to me. I would love to either help you find those people or critique your picture.

Dinner Parties

My friend Lana loves to throw parties. Dinner parties are her favorite.

Invite people over to your house once a month and have an interesting dinner party. Dinner parties of four to ten can be big. Remember, spending quality time with people is how you build deeper relationships. When you have them at your table, and you talk about interesting things, you learn a lot about someone. Also, you can choose who you want to invite and make sure there is a connection with the other people. They need to meet each other to do business or to do charity too. You always know people who need to know other people, so get them together. [1]

The party can be swanky or very casual. It can be a dinner you cook, cater, or a just watch a football game.

Some great ideas are:

- Cinco de Mayo dinner with Mexican food.
- Christmas Party with drinks and appetizers where everyone brings a gag gift.
- Spring Fling dinner party where you cook your favorite meats on the grill and eat outside.
- Any dinner party where you provide the main course and have everyone bring a side or appetizer.

---

[1] "Your Guide to the Art of Gathering," Priya Parker, accessed September 28, 2023, https://www.priyaparker.com/.

Mark holds a Client Appreciation Party every year. He sends out invitations to his top clients *and* top referral givers. He follows up with calls to ensure they received the invite. At the time of the party, he has made contact three to four times with everyone on the list. Having the party itself just gives you a reason to call people several times.

Farming

Real estate agents call it farming.[1] It means you take a certain neighborhood or community and you own it. You send out mailers to that neighborhood regularly. You knock on doors in that neighborhood, so you know each person individually. You sponsor events, like tennis and swim meets, in that neighborhood.

What are you farming? You should farm a local real estate company office nearby if you are a mortgage loan officer. You should farm the neighborhood you live in if you are a real estate agent. You should farm local mortgage companies if you are an insurance agent or a real estate closing attorney.

You should farm a local golf club or high-end neighborhood if you are a financial advisor. You should farm the local park if you are a local sporting goods retailer or own a restaurant where kids can come after games.

So, pick a neighborhood, a community, or a group of people, and farm the heck out of them. The object is to be known as "the person in the know" in that farm.

- Knock on the door to meet them in person. I made it a priority to know all the business owners in the downtown area of my community. The reason is I can send them business. When someone does a loan with me, I want them to ask me for referrals. The more referrals I give the more I receive. I tell the owners that when I do a loan for someone, I ask them how I can help. Do you need a caterer for your

---

1 Aaron Kardell, "14 Real Estate Farming Ideas & Techniques," HomeSpotter Blog, February 19, 2022, https://blog.homespotter.com/2019/12/14/real-estate-farming-ideas/.

Christmas party or a date night place that's really cool? I know the answers and can hook them up with the owner which makes it extra special for both of them.
- Email them. When you are door-knocking, you can ask for their business card. You want to use the email address to send out any news pertaining to them and the area they live in.
- Social media. Friend them and like or comment on their posts. That way they know you are watching and care.
- Offer services or connections. If they are going out of town, offer to pick up their mail or make sure any packages that are delivered are not piling up. If it is a business, offer to feature them in your newsletter or write a nice post about what they do.
- Send useful information. Always send them information about the neighborhood or about the business or the town that is useful. What's going on at so-and-so location or what the community is doing for Halloween.
- Be active politically. Show up at council or government meetings and build relationships with government officials. People will have a problem in your farm, and you want to be able to get them to the right person in government.
- Pick an area where no one has more than 25 percent of the market share. It will take you twice as long to get established as that person already has the branding and name recognition in place. You will be fighting an uphill battle.

If you are a real estate agent and have a new listing, use the "ten-ten-twenty" rule. Make forty copies of your listing flyer. Go to the ten neighbors on each side of your new listing and the twenty across the street. Knock on their door, introduce yourself, and ask them if they know anyone interested in moving into their neighborhood. Give them a copy of the flyer and let them know you have a new listing and would appreciate any help they could give you in selling the property. Some people will not be interested in helping you and want you to go away. That's okay, rejection is part of sales. But some people will be blown away because no other agent is doing this. Your sellers will love this!

My second entrepreneurial endeavor was the recycling business. This was before Earth Day had really caught on. In the late '80s and early '90s, people were starting to talk about recycling. I decided that would be a business I could start. No one was picking up recycling material at the curb. So, I bought a truck and some bins and started farming neighborhoods. I was the first person I knew of to do that in my area. At the time, it would only work if I charged to pick it up and most people were not recycling yet. The theory I had was to find a person I knew in several areas and offer to pick their recycling up for free if they would introduce me to their neighbors. Boy, did that work well. The funny thing was, my friends hated letting me pick up for free while charging the neighbors, so they all offered to pay too. But once I started and I was in a neighborhood, I would do door hangers and talk to folks who were out in the yard. It worked. Farming really works—mainly because no one does it. No one wants to "press the flesh" to get to know people.

Brian Henson does mailers and puts extra chewing gum and says, "I go the extra mile" or "Band-aids heal your real estate problems" Or "Advil—I'll fix your real estate headaches." It makes his current customers laugh and call him to say hi and tell him how funny he is.

Courtney Lott, real estate agent, likes to get with her customers on which neighborhoods work for them. She works with them to decide what price range and which neighborhoods have the right amenities they want. She then farms that neighborhood with a mailer, telling the homeowners she has a customer interested in their house and that neighborhood. She has found that she usually gets a few responses but, more importantly, she usually gets a person interested in listing their house with her.

As part of Edward Jones's training program, they require their new financial advisors to go door knocking within a certain radius of their local offices. It's a great way to meet local residents and business owners.

FORD and HEFE

Do you want to get better at conversation?

When you meet someone new and strike up a conversation, ask them about their FORD. [1]

F=Family
O=Occupation
R=Recreation
D=Dreams

If you get to dreams, you have a really good, deep conversation going! [2]

HEFE is another technique and this one is better when you are not really interested in what they do but just want to be a great conversationalist. [3]

H=Hobbies
E=Entertainment
F=Food
E=Environment

---

1 Jim Ries, "HOW TO USE THE FORD METHOD TO GET MORE CLIENTS," MDtechcouncil, January 13, 2022, https://www.mdtechcouncil.com/tcm/memberPOV/how-to-use-the-ford-method-to-get-more-clients/#:~:text=FORD%20is%20an%20acronym%20that,teach%20to%20other%20business%20developers.
2 David A. Morin et al., "How to Use the F.O.R.D Method (with Example Questions)," SocialSelf, July 22, 2021, https://socialself.com/blog/ford-method/.
3 Oddfix, "Why Ford Is Bullshit & Why Hefe Is Way Better.," Reddit, 2018, https://www.reddit.com/r/socialskills/comments/aep2h8/why_ford_is_bullshit_why_hefe_is_way_better/.

Another thing I do is the Bowling Ball. When you are at a party, you will notice people gather in small groups of two to five and stand in little clusters all around the party. When I see this, I pretend to be a bowling ball. I just bust up the pins like I am a bowling ball and insert myself into the conversation. When you do this, you have to be aware that some people are having a private conversation and usually these are groups of two, but most people are just talking about nothing. So, bowl right into the conversation and add something. Tell them it's lonely out there and you want to know if you can join their tribe. Tell them they are the most interesting people in the room, and you want to be interesting too.

Grow Your Referrals

I'm a big believer in giving out referrals. I have found that the more I give, the more I get. The referral Gods shine on me!

When I meet somebody, I want to be their national sales manager. That means I want to tell everybody I meet about them. It means I have them entered into my phone in a way that allows me to look them up on the spot and "Direct Connect" them instantly.

I want to be Santa Claus for them today. Everybody loves Christmas because you get gifts. Give the person in front of you a gift. I want to send them as much business as I can, as soon as I can. When you do that, it creates a WOW in others.

You are seen as a GIVER and not a TAKER.

When I refer people, I get more business. I do not necessarily get a direct referral from the person I'm helping, but for some reason, I get referrals from others. It was hard to do this at first, but the more I do it, the more business I get. Just giving to others not only pumps you up, but reciprocity kicks in. That's how I've grown my business over the last twenty-five years.

The key is to go into every interaction with another person looking for a way to refer them business or people who could help them. But sometimes you can use what's going on in your business as a way to call others and tell them about something cool going on that their friends should take advantage of. I don't use this often but sometimes people just need to know what you know.

A few months ago, I was seeing rates lower than I've ever seen them. Now's a great time to refinance your home. I can use this as an excuse to call people. I could say, "If you have a mortgage and you plan on staying there awhile, and your rate is over 4 percent, you need to call your mortgage guy because it's a fantastic opportunity for you to refinance." Notice I said *call your mortgage guy*. I do this on purpose so they know I'm not asking them for business but recommending they investigate refinancing because it could help them.

So do what you can for people, help them as much as you can, and they'll turn around and help you.

I read this article recently and want to share it with you so you understand it's not just my opinion. This is about mortgage loan officers, but the same theory works for all of us who are B2C.

> "Recently, MGIC surveyed 144 loan officers who originated at least $5 million in loan volume in a 6-month period to find out some of the secrets to their success. Unsurprisingly, referrals were a hot topic – and 96% of those surveyed said that real estate agents are one of their best sources for generating referrals.
>
> Here's what we learned about the top 3 ways that loan officers build relationships and generate referrals with real estate agents.
>
> *81% of Top Loan Officers Make Referrals to Earn Referrals*
>
> It just makes intuitive sense: if you refer customers to real estate agents, they're more likely to refer their own buyers to you. But don't make indiscriminate recommendations just to get your foot in the door – if your borrowers have a bad experience with a real estate agent, it won't reflect well on you. A strong referral relationship burnishes the reputation of both parties. And a borrower who has a great experience overall will be more likely to recommend everyone involved.
>
> That was true for my family (authors!) – when we bought our last home, our agent referred us to a loan officer. He was ready and available, extremely easy to communicate with. Since we had such a great experience during our purchase process, we reached back out when we were interested in refinancing and recommended him to others.
>
> *42% of Top Loan Officers Attend Events*
>
> Events – in-person or virtual – can help loan officers build a deeper relationship with real estate agents. Whether it's lunch, coffee date, training session, happy hour, loan

closing or golf event (just to name a few), it's a chance to make a connection and prove your value. Here's what our survey respondents said:

- **53% of the originators we surveyed attend one loan closing per week.** One respondent told me: "I attend closings because they help me to build relationships. I get to spend time with clients as well as real estate agents. It's such an exciting and memorable time for most. And being able to make a lasting impression can create repeat business."

- **23% of loan officers attend open houses once every few months.** While less popular than loan closings, some loan officers touted open houses as a great way to spend valuable one-on-one time with a real estate agent

- **Training events are a great way to meet real estate agents and strengthen relationships. Continuing education, whether for formal credits or not, is an important part of professional development in any industry. Your referral partners will remember you as the loan officer who brought them that value**

21% of Top Loan Officers Connect through Social Media

Looking for a way to reach a lot of real estate agents at once? Try social media. Posting relevant content can help you stay top-of-mind with referral partners. The most popular platforms for the originators we surveyed were:

- Facebook (60%)
- LinkedIn (27%)
- Instagram (20%)

While less popular, some survey respondents reported success with YouTube: 'Instead of making calls and doing happy hours, I use YouTube to tell stories about what my team and I have done for customers that week. It allows my subscribers to see my creative side. Sure, it requires planning and work, but it keeps me current with people in the industry.'

These concepts may not seem ground-breaking – but the classics are classics for a reason. Are you actively pursuing these tried-and-true real estate referral strategies today?"[1]

I believe the same holds true in your industry. There are certain people you should call on and certain ways your industry experts build a referral business. However, most people forget about the power of their sphere of influence. I realized years ago that the best way for me to send real estate agents' business was to know more people in my town. The more I know, the more I have asking me for recommendations and some of those are for real estate agents. The same is true for you. The more people you know in your town the more people you can connect. If everybody you are building relationships with is in the same industry, then you want to have as many referrals.

In my town, there are a lot of people moving here who are "not from around here." The newbies don't have deep relationships in the community and when they meet guys like me who know a lot of people, they ask me for referrals. Since I give out a lot of referrals, I create a WOW for not only the person who needs someone but also with the person I referred.

A young man called me one day and asked if he could meet me. He was interested in running for the US House of Representatives. His main concern was talking to people who were not only Republican, but wealthy because it was going to take a lot of money. I offered to help. So, with him in my office, I started calling the folks I felt fit the bill. What I didn't realize is how it gave me a reason to talk to some of the wealthiest people in town. Normally, those folks would not have a reason to talk to a mortgage guy because they pay cash for their homes. But a few of them were interested and I got to give them my name for anyone they may know interested in buying a home. Out of that, one guy who was a residential developer called me back and asked me to do the loans on a subdivision he was building— ended up getting several loans out of that and the candidate got a little money too.

---

1 1. Stephanie Budnik, "Loan Officer Hub Blog," Loan Officer Hub: Strategies, June 7, 2021, https://loanofficerhub.com/blog/3-ways-top-loan-officers-connect-with-real-estate-agents.

Sales Pitch

Rehearse and record your sales pitch on why people should do business with you. Then, test it on someone who can give you great feedback.

This is one of the hardest things to do. You need to be able to explain to others why they should do business with you. The bigger part is you need to believe it yourself.

I still struggle with this a lot myself. I came up with the idea that I would explain to the potential customers what I think they need to hear. I thought my story would be important to them.

If I have a customer that is solely focused on price, I tell them that I own the company and that I can do it for free if I want to or I can lose money if I want to. But, if I did it that way, I would not be in business for the last thirty years.

"Mr. Customer, if price is the only thing you are interested in, then I am not your guy. I value others who have expertise and knowledge over price. I'm sure you are not the cheapest price at what you do."

If they don't know enough about me to trust me, I explain to them I have been in business for over twenty-five years and am the past president of the Mortgage Brokers Association. My company, for several years, was in the top five mortgage companies in Georgia by the *Atlanta Business Chronicle*. I have sat on numerous boards and have been a member of the Alpharetta Rotary Club for over thirty years. That usually lets them know I am a player.

When they are buying their first home and are scared, I tell them the story of when I bought my first home. I didn't know what questions to ask or if I was getting a good deal or not. If they have time, I want to give them a quick mortgage 101 class on what takes place and how the timeline usually works. I want them to understand all the players in the transaction, like me, the real estate agent, appraiser, and attorney. I explain the things to look out for and what they don't need to worry about. After the 101, I usually have them in the palm of my hand because no one else is doing that for them. Not even their parents.

Lots of people have an elevator speech and it makes me want to vomit. Don't do it.

Make the conversation about the person in front of you and not about you. Most elevator pitches are too vague and use too many industry buzzwords. People get lost in all that bull. Try to figure out what they need to hear and answer it as directly as you can.

Ultimately, if you are doing your marketing right, you won't have to give too many sales pitches. You want someone to do that for you. That's called a referral!

Video

To use video to build your brand, there are a few key strategies you can implement. Here are some ideas:

• Create a personal introductory video

Use a personal introduction video to introduce yourself to potential clients and give them a glimpse into your personality and expertise. This video could include information about your background, what you bring to the table in your particular industry, and the types of properties or clients you specialize in.

• Highlight local expertise

It's important to showcase your knowledge of the local area you serve. Consider creating videos that highlight your favorite local spots, the best schools in the area, or other notable features that make your community unique.

- If you are in the real estate industry, showcase properties with video tours

Use video tours to showcase properties and give potential buyers a virtual tour. You can point out features, highlight the best views, and emphasize any other selling points of the property.

• Provide educational content

Creating educational content focused on your particular industry can help you stand out as an expert in your field. Consider creating videos that cover topics such as market trends, financing options, insurance risks, etc.

• Promote your brand on social media

Use video to promote your brand on social media platforms such as Facebook, Instagram, and LinkedIn. Share your personal introduction video, property tours, and informative videos on social media to reach a wider audience and build your brand awareness.

These are just a few ideas for using video to build your brand. By being creative and leveraging video to showcase your expertise and properties, you can establish yourself as a trusted and knowledgeable real estate professional.

Video marketing can be highly effective for a number of reasons:

1. Virtual tours: Video marketing allows real estate agents to create virtual tours of properties, which can be especially beneficial for out-of-town buyers or busy clients who may not have the time to attend a physical showing. Virtual tours give viewers a clear sense of the property layout and features, which can help to increase interest and generate leads. Insurance agents can use virtual tours of homes that include where smoke alarms and fire extinguishers should be located.

2. Engage clients: Insurance agents, financial advisors, and real estate agents can use video marketing to engage clients and provide helpful tips and information. For example, you might create videos that cover topics like "Tips for First-Time Homebuyers," "How to Do a 401K Roll Over," or "Local Market Trends." These videos can be shared on social media or email newsletters to build your brand and provide value to potential clients.

3. Showcase expertise: By creating informative videos, you can also establish yourself as an expert in your field. This can help to build trust with potential clients and provide an edge over competitors. Financial advisors can send videos of trends in the stock or bond market.

4. Increased engagement: Videos tend to have higher engagement rates than other forms of content. By using video, you can capture the attention of potential clients and keep them engaged for longer periods of time.

Overall, video marketing can be a highly effective tool for anyone looking to build their brand, showcase properties, and provide valuable information to potential clients.

Points System

This system was pioneered by Al Granum for life insurance salespeople.

My friends in that industry say to make sales a process and not to worry about the outcome. If you do, you take the emotion out of the sales process. Sales is a numbers game. We learn from other industries.

Here is how the game is played. The whole idea is to get one hundred points a month.

You get half a point for a qualified prospect, one that has a certain level of earnings, is married, or sold a business.

You get one point for an in-person meeting. It's a fact-finding mission or a series of questions about the prospect to discover their needs and pains—basically, you know everything about them. Take notes and put them on a form.

You get another point if you close the sale. Ten-three-one means you call ten prospects, get three meetings, and have one closed sale.

Have brainstorming sessions with your peer group. Sit in a room with other salespeople and report what you have done for the month. Have others critique you on how you are talking with your clients. This usually creates friendly competition among the group.

If you are a rookie and starting a new sales job, you need to have three hundred names you can call when you start. Then ask those three hundred who they know.

If you are a real estate agent, when you list a house, ask the seller to introduce you to ten people in the neighborhood.

If you are a mortgage loan officer or insurance agent, then ask a real estate agent who else you should meet in their office.

Workman Success Systems has a system called Daily Success Habits. You accrue points by making calls, going on appointments, and having closings. It helps you keep track of how you are spending your day and holds you accountable to yourself.

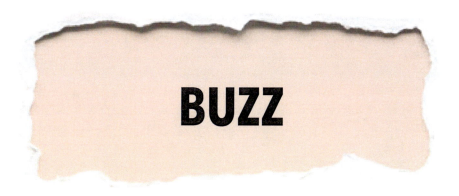

BUZZ

What's Your Buzz?

"Buzz" is what others say about you. It's the buzz part of word of mouth that makes you sizzle. Buzz is the thing that is different and unique about you. It's what makes me want to tell others the cool thing I just learned about you, from you.

We love to talk about each other and when you give people something good or interesting to talk about, they will tell even more people. What I'd like to teach you is how to make yourself more colorful and interesting to others so they will talk about you in a way that will make you money. Buzz needs ammunition. Learning how to arm yourself for different conversations is critical to being buzz-worthy. People tell others about you because they are impressed by you and believe that what they know about you relates to their own lives.

I became interested in buzz when I realized that when two people meet and talk about a third party, they use buzz. In other words, if you meet me and then go home and tell your spouse about me, everything you say is my buzz. It's what is cool—and maybe not so cool—about me. The interesting thing is that most of the information that is buzzed about me comes directly from me, or from what has been said about me by another person.

If someone asks what I do, and all I say is I'm a speaker, they don't have much to buzz about me later. The sad thing is that this is what most people do. However, if I say I'm a speaker and I have spent a good portion of my life studying why people refer other people, and that while studying that, I came up with some different ideas about how we get referral business, that might get more attention. I could go on to say I changed the way I sell to a way of getting people to want to buy from me. And I do this by spending time with people to help them get where they want to go. I literally seek out strangers, as well as friends, and spend a good portion of every day trying to help them succeed. When I do this, almost every time, they want to help me in return.

This is where you have to be very good at painting a really clear picture of what you need so that when they see that picture, it will remind them of you and they will send business your way. I used this philosophy to become one of the top mortgage loan officers in the state of Georgia and in the process, I learned that if you help people instead of hustle them, not only is business more fun but life is too. So now I travel around the country teaching others to do the same thing through speaking engagements and workshops for corporations.

What I have learned to do is give people something to go home and talk about. And it has to be a lot more interesting than "I'm a speaker."

If you are in a business where you need customers to buy from you, consider your buzz. Everybody has it but not everybody uses it right. A financial advisor needs buzz that he can make your money grow. An insurance agent needs to show how knowledgeable he is in making sure you have just the right amount of insurance. A mortgage guy has good rates and knows how to get you approved. A preacher cares about your personal circumstances with sickness or death or marriage. An attorney wins cases. A CPA helps grow your business and minimize your tax burden. A professor has spent time and was successful in the field he is teaching. A doctor has good bedside manners and is viewed by his peers as really knowing his specialty. A restaurant has the best of a certain kind of food or dish. A clothing store owner goes to cool places on buying trips to get you stuff no one else will be wearing. A hair stylist understands your type of hair and lifestyle, etc.

You see, buzz travels fast through networks of people and they trust that the information is correct because they are friends. Buzz is 40 to 60 percent of the reason people know about you and your business. Think about the last three items you purchased. I'll bet at least one of them was recommended by another person.

But buzz can be bad too. So, read my book *What's Your BUZZ?* to learn more.

Also, watch my video on *What's Your BUZZ?* [1]

---

[1] Steve Beecham, "Whats Your Buzz," video.stevebeecham.com, accessed September 28, 2023, https://video.stevebeecham.com/media/motivational-speaking-speaking-promo-videos-whats-your-buzz-369636.

Be Santa Claus

Everyone loves Santa Claus because he brings you gifts. What happens if you become Santa for everyone you meet? If you do, a lot of people will have great things to say about you.

Every time I meet a new person, the main thing I want to leave that conversation with is how I can help. How can I introduce them to someone they think is cool? In order to do that, you have to dig deep into the conversation to learn two things.

First, what is the perfect customer for them? Who could I send them to that they would think, "WOW"? Who would rock their world? A financial advisor wants to meet someone with money. But what kind of wealthy person? One that sold his/her company or one who is retiring and wants to roll over their IRA. They probably want to meet both, but which one do they get excited about? That's the one I want to introduce them to.

A real estate agent wants to meet someone who wants to sell their house. But do they want to sell a farm or a high-rise condo more?

My CPA told me she liked small-business people. One day, my veterinarian called and said he needed a new accountant who understood small business. I hooked them up and they are both happy. BAM. Santa strikes!

The second thing you need to know is what their favorite hobbies or favorite pastimes are. Everyone has something they like to do after work or on the weekends. Maybe they mountain bike or ride motorcycles. They could be into baking or reading history books. It doesn't matter what it is, but you need to find out.

Why?

Because one day, you are going to meet someone else who does or is interested in doing the same thing. When you meet them, you can introduce the two. If you do, they both say WOW. I tell the story of a guy I met who was into mountain biking and then a week later I met another guy who wanted to get into mountain biking. He said he didn't know if he needed a $500 bike or a $10,000 bike. I connected the two and the pro helped the amateur.[1]

---

[1] Steve Beecham, "Casey Cunningham Podcast," video.stevebeecham.com, accessed September 28, 2023, https://video.stevebeecham.com/media/motivational-speaking-speaking-promo-videos-casey-cunningham-podcast-460837.

Do you send out a newsletter? I send an e-newsletter once a week, and it's one of the best practices for my business. I've been doing it for at least fifteen years.

I want to tell you a little bit about what I have learned about newsletters. First of all, a lot of people don't send them out often and then they get complaints when they do. And the main reason is because you're sending out what I call a *Fortune* magazine-type newsletter. You're sending out stuff about the accounting industry or the stock industry or the real estate industry. And I don't need to see that every week. Your local industry-type email newsletter is fine, but it won't get you big business. Do send it out if it is free but know you will get a lot of deletes. If I'm not in the market for those services, then I'm not going to read your newsletter. What people really want in a newsletter is the *National Enquirer*. They want to know about the gossip that's going on in town. They want to know about things they don't already know about, like what is going on in the building where Kmart used to be or who is building that new house that's so big and pretty.

Everyone would read that newsletter if you did it right. You must do a newsletter that's a little bit between a *Fortune* magazine and a gossip column. What I came up with is sort of like a *People* magazine newsletter. I want to be the go-to source every week of what's going on in my town. Are there festivals, are there functions? Is someone selling Girl Scout cookies, are the Boy Scouts trying to raise money to do a local project? Is somebody having a cancer ball or is there some sort of ball going on to raise money for charity? I want to be the social chairman in my village. The great thing about my newsletter is that everyone I meet, I can send my newsletter to because everyone wants to read it.

They won't delete it. They won't say you're spamming me. If you're sending out a newsletter, that's approved by your company, then you have to go with that. But, it's so generic and it works because your name is in the inbox. If you could find something that can make your newsletter different, do it.

A friend of mine I was coaching asked me for some assistance on doing a newsletter. I asked him what he was really into. He said craft beers. I asked, "Well, why don't you just do a newsletter about craft beers, craft beer festivals all over the Southeast? How you make craft beer? Do tours of distilleries. Every time, no matter where you are, you can ask people, 'Hey, man, do you like craft beers?' If they say yes, ask them if they would like to get a copy of your newsletter."

A friend of mine is into music. He started doing a newsletter on all the local music scene that was happening around Atlanta. The bands, the people, and the venues all wanted to get his newsletter. At the bottom of his newsletter, he just happened to mention that if you needed your computer repaired, he would love to help.

A real estate friend of mine and I schemed on a newsletter for her. She had one of those yappy dogs she carried around in a purse. One of her problems was restaurants would not let her bring the dog inside. I urged her to start writing a newsletter about the places that were dog-friendly. I told her to take time to take a picture of her with the owner and mention that the restaurant loves dogs and that you could get a dog treat. Before long, others were telling her where to go, and restaurateurs were asking her to come do a story on them. At the bottom of the newsletter, she just happened to mention she was a real estate agent.

By doing something unique and different, it gives you an opportunity to send your newsletter and not worry about getting deleted. The whole idea behind a newsletter is really not so much the content as it is the fact that your name is showing up in their inbox as frequently as you can. So, think about a newsletter that you can put out that's like a *People* magazine. That's a little bit about who you are in the community. It must be something that people want to look at every week. If you have any questions about that, don't hesitate to call me. Newsletter, get one.

Cathy was referred to me by her neighbor. I did a refinance on her home and after we closed, I added Cathy to my newsletter. Several weeks later, she called to ask if I would put information about a charity ball she was working on in my newsletter. The next several weeks we had it in my newsletter. Because of that, she sold tickets to her charity ball. She was so excited that I helped her get the word out, that when it came time for her daughter to buy her first house, guess who got the call? Me.

This guy Mike called me, "You don't know me, but I have been following you for twenty years. My wife received your newsletter. We moved to California and are moving back. I am calling you because I need a mortgage."

Mark had a past client named Jay. He had not spoken to him (shame on Mark) in ten years, but Jay received his newsletter. Jay called him when they were ready to sell and buy a new home. Mark made money on two commissions.

It works people!

Join More Clubs!

Over the years, I have interviewed a lot of salespeople. I love asking people where most of their business comes from. They always say referrals. When I press for more information, I usually discover that most of their business comes from one resource.

Most real estate agents will say they get business from their neighborhood or the school where their kids attend. Insurance guys might say the Rotary or the Kiwanis Club. Some investment advisors might say their church or the chamber of commerce. The problem is they usually only name one organization. Most of their business comes from one place.

However, when I interview highly successful salespeople, they usually will name two or three of the above. The rock-star salespeople usually are members of all of them!

Like my friend Trummie, one of the most successful insurance agents in the country. He told me he was a member of Rotary, involved in his church, sat on a board of his college, was the board chair of a state department, was still involved as an alumnus of his fraternity, and was on the board of a local bank. His wife was in the local women's club and a board member of a nonprofit.

If you want to double your business, just join another club! If you want to triple your business join two more clubs. If you want to be the envy of your peers join as many as you can.

Yes, it will take up some time, but if your job is to produce and you are successful, there will always be a way to hire more people to handle your volume.

Really it is just that simple, join more groups and you will get more business.

I was asked to be on the board of my local Chamber of Commerce. One of the issues we were having in my town at the time was there were a lot of new folks moving to our area. People who did not grow up around here. They would ask questions like why is there no sewer over here or why does the county police this part of town and the city this part of town. I decided we needed a class on what was going on in our town. A class that would introduce you and teach you all the stuff about what makes a city/county government work. So, we set up what later became a chamber leadership class. When we started, it put me in a position to go talk to the county water and sewer people. I met with the police department and the power company. All the local municipalities and utilities along with elected officials all agreed to help teach the class. It was a huge success. The great part for me is that I got to meet a lot of people I would have never gotten to meet. People who wanted to contribute and help grow awareness in our community. Over the years I have done lots of loans just from those connections.

See the chapter on "Small Groups" to know how to make the most of a new club when you join it.

Levels of Introduction

Did you know there are different ways you can be introduced? I never really thought about that. And then I started reading some stories and I started gathering some information and learning about the different levels of introduction. So, for instance, if I meet you somewhere and you say, "Hey, Steve, I need an artist to draw something on my wall."

And I say, "Okay, call my friend, Jim, here's his phone number." That is the lowest level of introduction.

The highest level of introduction is you say, "I need an artist."

And I say, "Look, I'm going to get with my friend, Jim, and I'm going to set up lunch to introduce you to him." That's really the way Jim would like to be introduced to you as an artist. And now I'm there, brokering the conversation. How powerful is that?

And in our mind, we say, "I don't really want to do that because it takes time for me to set that up and do all that." But, I think you're missing the point if you're thinking that way. If you just give someone a name and a number, there's no guarantee that your friend knows this other person called them. You might run into them later and say, "Hey, did Sally call you?" And they say, "No, I never heard from Sally." So, if you set up a meeting and you do that, then I get to promote Sally and I get to promote Jim. And that adds to them wanting to reciprocate to me so that if I ever need them to introduce *me* to somebody, they're more than willing to do it. And they'll probably buy me lunch because I did it for them.

If you want people to introduce you a certain way, then you need to introduce other people that same way. Your best level of introduction is when you set up the meeting. The other thing I learned was that when I refer someone to another person, I used to just give them their name and number like we did earlier. Well, I've quit doing that.

So, what I do now when Sally says, "Yes, I need an artist."

I say, "I know a great artist. I'm going to have him call you. Would that be OK with you?"

"Yes, that'd be great."

So now I call my friend, the artist, and say, "Hey, my friend Sally is looking for an artist. I've told her about you. She's expecting your phone call. Here's her phone number, call her."

Now that person will call because they think this person is waiting on their phone call, which they are. But I also get to make sure my friend knows I was giving him a referral. There's no gray area. He knows I called him and I did everything I could to get this piece of business to him.

So don't give out names and numbers anymore. If you really want to gain a lot of traction with referrals, I want you to call the person and say the other person's expecting your phone call. Please do that. It'll change everything for you. And try to give away referrals by having lunch or dinner or coffee or three-way conversations on the phone. Any way you can get those two to three people together is better than giving somebody a name or number.

Most real estate agents are accustomed to giving out referrals to certain vendors to their clients for housing needs. Mark has a lot of his past clients and sphere of influence contacts call to ask if he knows a painter, electrician, handyman, etc. He used to give out the number of specific vendors but now he connects via a three-way call. His past clients get WOWed every time!

Small Groups

One of the big problems I see with people in my local community is they'll join the Rotary Club or the chamber of commerce, and then six months or a year later, they'll say, I didn't get anything out of it. Guess what, that's true.

The problem is they don't realize the strength in groups is in the small group. So, what I always tell people is if you're going to join the chamber, that's fine. Join the chamber. But you have to get somebody in the chamber to put you in a smaller group.

It's kind of like church. You know, if you just went to church and sat in the pew, and you listened to the sermon and you went home, how many people are you going to meet? Not many. This is why they want you to sign the visitor log, so they can contact you to get an understanding of your needs. Now, if you go to church and you get into Sunday school class, that's a smaller group of people you start to meet quicker.

If you go and you get into a Bible study, which is an even smaller group, of maybe five or ten, then you get to meet people.

So, what happens is, as you meet people in the Sunday school class you see them at church, and then they introduce you to their friends. And that's how you build your pyramid. They group certain people you know. Same thing with the chamber of commerce. You join a group—they might be the group that goes out and tries to get more people to come into the chamber. It might be the group that's involved in politics of what's going on around town.

And so, those smaller groups meet more frequently. They'll meet once a month or every two weeks, and there's five or ten of you in the room. And over a period of time, you get to know those people better. And because you get to know them better when you're in the larger group, you now have more people you can hook up. And now they can introduce you to more people as well.

So anytime you're going to join an organization, try to figure out how you can get into a smaller group of that organization, because that allows you to meet more people quicker.

Visiting

I want to talk to you about a Deep South concept that I call Visiting. In the good old days, you would just go over to someone's house, usually not invited, and sit on the porch and just catch up and talk. This was done mostly on Sundays when people were home. It may be a family walking down the street you invite to your front porch. Or, you jumped into the car to go to your aunts for dinner and then just stop by and see how Charlie and June were doing. I remember it and it was fun!

If you are like me, you need to meet new people, right? You can't grow a business unless you meet new people. Well, guess what? So does everybody else in business. We all need to meet new people.

One of my favorite things to do is to take somebody who's in a fairly similar business and go visit other people. In the mortgage business, this might be an insurance agent, a closing attorney, or a real estate agent. Invite them to lunch and after you eat, go visit people near where you had lunch.

If I were with an insurance agent, I would ask him to introduce me to one or two people he knew in the area. We would just drop by for a visit. It is always easy because the person already knows him. It might even be a customer of his. Then, I would introduce him to one or two people I know. I would drive my friend to a business somebody I know owns, and we would go in there and I'd say, "Hey, Jack, I want you to meet my buddy, Johnny. He's an insurance agent. Hey, Johnny, Jack sells IT services." I'll make the introduction for them. Each of my two friends get to meet somebody new.

It works like a charm. He meets my friends and I meet his

friends. The best time to do this is on a Friday afternoon. People are a little bit more relaxed.

Then, we get back in the car and I get my insurance guy to take me to somebody he knows that I don't. Now, he walks in and introduces me to somebody. And when you do that, you're going to have a longer, deeper, better conversation with this new person. You're going to get to know them a little better than if you just met them at a chamber of commerce meeting, or if you cold-called them.

Look out in your world and see who you need to go visiting with, then meet for lunch. Somebody in a business that's kind of looking for the same customer you are. Take them and introduce them to one, two, or three people they don't know. And they do the same thing for you. It's the best, most powerful introduction you can have.

Visiting. Try it. You'll love it.

Real estate agent Kelly Finley decided to visit old businesses in her town. She researched which ones had been around for a long time and then went to visit them. She then asked if she could do a story or a post on them. The post was about surviving the changes that occurred over the years and the history of the business. By doing this, she spotlighted the business but also got to meet the people. They were thrilled and she was too.

Who Can I Introduce You To?

Next time you are with someone, and they are in business, sales, or somebody that's looking for customers, you want to ask them who you can introduce them to. This is huge for anyone who needs a customer. No one ever asks them that question. Most of us are trying to figure out if there is anything in there for ourselves. Flip the script. Be the giver, not the taker.

Is there anybody that might be in my network, maybe some of my customers or friends, that could use what you sell? I call this "Bringing your Assets, not your Agenda." Everybody and everything you know is an asset. Open your rolodex to them. Let them know you have five thousand Facebook friends and seven thousand people in your database that you could connect them to. I go as far as to let them know I have them categorized by what they do so I can look them up quickly.

Who can I introduce you to today or right now? The least I'm going to do is share contact information, but if I really want to WOW them, I call the other person right then and there or I do a three-way call if I have them on the phone with me. See the previous chapter on "Direct Connect."

I learned that if I help them grow their business, there's a good chance they're going to help me grow my business. Givers get! Give it away! You will be blown away by how many people will return the favor. This week I did a speech for a business organization. One of the guys from the audience reached out to me the next day to meet for coffee. We met and I poured into him all the contacts I could. After about an hour he asked me how he could help me. I mentioned I needed to meet more real estate agents in his part of town. That afternoon, he sent me five LinkedIn connections with introductions to some really good agents. Next week I am having lunch with two of them. That's what happens.

Nobody is calling me on a regular basis saying, "Beech, who can I introduce you to today?" That's what I really want. Right? If I want to grow my business, I need to meet new people. But nobody does that very often. But I wish they did. That's how I know it is a great thing to do for others. What happens if you become that person and you say to your friends, every time you are with them, "Who can I introduce you to today?" They will reciprocate!

Spend today thinking about who you can call that's a friend of yours, who's in business, who you can say, "Hey, who can I introduce you to today? I'd love to help you make a sale today. I'd love to help you make an introduction today." If you do that, you will never have anyone hang up on you! Use that phrase when you cold-call or meet someone new. It immediately makes them like you and they learn you are a person of significance in the meantime. You know people!

Who can I introduce you to?

Breakroom Sticky

I know that sounds goofy. Breakroom sticky is the way to go when you need other people in your office to help you grow your business. I came up with this idea when I was working with the CEO of a bank. The bank was fairly new in town. The CEO was trying to meet as many small businesspeople in town as he could. So, I came up with the idea that every day he would go into the breakroom, he would take a sticky pad, and write who he wanted to meet that day. Then, he would put the sticky notes on the wall. There were about eight or nine employees at this one-horse bank branch. Some were loan officers and others were administrative folks. Each day, the CEO would put a new category of business on the sticky note. Things like plumber, electrician, and divorce attorney.

Everybody said, "What's that about?"

He said, "Well, I want to meet a plumber. Some of our customers might need a plumber and I want to be able to refer them to somebody."

A couple of the girls said, "Well, I know a plumber."

He said, "Well, if you introduce me to a plumber that owns his own company we could refer our customers to, I'll take you to lunch and pay for it. Anywhere you want to go in town—and I'll pay for the plumber's lunch too." He continued, "I promise I'm not going to try to sell them on anything with the bank. I just want to meet him because I need a good referral source for a plumber." So, he started doing that and every day he would change the sign from a plumber to an electrician and then to a real estate agent, whatever he was looking for.

About 75 percent of the time, somebody in the branch knew

somebody in that line of work and the employees started getting excited about it. Since he was buying lunch anywhere in town, they were able to go to all the different, cool places to eat. Plus he never pushed it. He just said, "I want to know you and know more about your business and how I can help."

After about a year of that, his business really started to grow because some of those contractors he focused on knew the builders who needed construction loans. Some knew the people who were going to need remodeling loans or knew the people who needed an equity line because they were going to put in a pool.

So, I want you to think about how you can use the breakroom sticky where you work, or maybe at your spouse's place of business, or maybe you can find somebody else who owns a business. A friend of yours might own an accounting business. Or maybe you're a real estate agent. You might go in and put a sticky note in there that says: Do you know anybody that's had a baby lately? Maybe they're going to need to buy a new house. Or do you know anybody who's graduated from college? I'll buy you both lunch.

It might be different, but it's fun. So, think about how you can use the breakroom sticky idea to advertise that you're looking to meet somebody because you want to send them business. Not because you want to *do* business, but because you want to *develop* that relationship with a person in that line of work, because you need somebody to refer.

So where are you going to put your breakroom sticky?

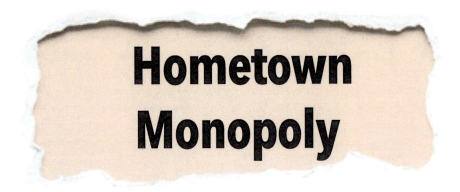

Hometown Monopoly

Here is a fun game to play to meet the important people in your town. Get an aerial map of your town or a portion of your town and blow it up. Stick it up on the wall in your office.

Then, start writing down each business that is in that area and who the owner is. The object is to meet as many owners of the businesses in your area as you can. If you don't know who the owner is, write it in yellow ink. If you know who owns a store, but not personally, then write it in red ink. When you meet the owner, write it in black ink.

Once you meet five new owners, reward yourself.

Then go about asking people who own the shoe or tire store. When they tell you, ask them to introduce you. Once you get a chance to meet them, "Bring your Assets, not your Agenda."

Make a List

Does making a list make a difference? I say it does. Highly successful people are really good at making lists. They are good at making lists of what they want to accomplish tomorrow or in the future.

Here's why it works. If you are going to Paris, you are going to make a list of all the places you want to see. Then, you make your list of to-dos: airfare, hotels, rental cars, tour guides, etc. You start looking into items in your list, you get a better understanding of how much things will cost, and decide if you are still in or not. Then action takes over. You pay for your airfare and book a hotel.

Once you start crossing off items on your list, then you start to see the destination. In this case, we get to Paris.

So, wherever you want to go in life, make a list of action items that will get you there. Start with the end in mind and work down from there. It helps you free up space in your brain.

Have goals and read that list every day.

Employee Appreciation Day

Write a letter to your employees and their family members thanking them for doing a good job. Heather Pastrick writes an appreciation note to her employees' spouses, saying thank you to their families for being supportive and allowing her to work with them. People need to feel your love. Employees need to know you care about them. If they do, they will run through a brick wall for you. Maybe send them a box of their favorite things—candies, hobbies, and items for spouses or kids. Maybe do it for Thanksgiving, it's a day to be thankful for them as employees.

Do the same thing for your customers. Your top 20 percent pay you the most money and are with you through thick and thin.

I throw a Christmas party every year and invite my past clients, sphere of influence, and employees.

Show thanks and gratitude toward those who support you!

Be Curious Like a Ten-Year-Old

Remember when you were ten years old and you would ask your parents questions like, "Dad, why is the sky blue?" or "Dad, how does an airplane fly?" or "Why does the ocean taste salty?"

Those conversations always spark long answers. They are not political or religious, they are just interesting stuff you don't know the answer to. What would it be like if you did that when you talked to others? These questions build relationships. No, you might not ask this on the first date, but you should sometime thereafter.

Curiosity leads to you wanting to know the answer to things you don't already know about, which then allows you to give that information to others. This builds your brand and your referrals. It gives you the internal power to have information that others might not have, which enhances your brand because you are knowledgeable.

Being curious also makes the conversation about them and not about you. I recently had a person wanting to talk to me about running for mayor of a local city. I met him for a beer and for an hour and a half he talked about himself. How great his accomplishments were and how everyone knew him. He then asked what I thought about him running for mayor. I told him he would lose. I said, "If you knock on my door and ask for my vote, then vomit all over me about your greatness and never ask me anything about what I think is good or bad about our city, then I will think you are a narcissist and won't vote for you." Do not be the person that is talking in a conversation. Be the one who is asking questions and wants to know more.

So, what happens if you start asking those curious questions?

- What do you do daily in your job? (This question allows you to dig deeper, to find out how much time they spend on stuff that matters versus stuff that does not. I want to help them spend more time on the fun stuff.)
- What's your superpower? (It could be they are a great listener or a turn-around artist. I want to know this because when I have a friend who is in trouble, I call the person with the superpower to get them out of trouble.)
- What do you do for fun? (Often, I find a person who has decided to start a new hobby and they don't know what equipment to buy or where to go to enjoy it. I want to introduce them to someone who is an expert in that hobby and help their hobby time grow.)
- Read any good books lately? (I read a lot, so I am always curious what new books are out there. This is mainly for my own self-interest.)
- What's your life purpose? (I only ask this after I have spent some time with someone. I usually ask this when I see them floundering and not living their most purposeful life. I am interested in this subject, so I really try to drill down and help them if they are not purposeful.)

In my town, I like to know about new developments. People will ask me what is going on in a local store or hotel. When I see city officials who might have the answer, I ask them questions about it. Once I have the answers, I repeat them to others. If I am at lunch, I can tell others what is going on there and how cool or not cool it is going to be. I let them know if the city is excited or not. It ultimately gives me street credibility that I know something they don't.

When I interview a person for a loan application, I have to ask them what they do for a living. Most people give you the normal stuff. They might work in IT for Google or in management for UPS. We all know that is very vague, so I try to drill down. "What specifically does that mean? I'm not an IT person, so what do you do on a daily basis? How did you learn that? What do you hope to do next or where would you like to end up?" When I do this with a customer, it takes me out of my loan officer role and puts me into a personal "I care" role.

Most people are afraid to cold call. So, don't! Be a person who wants to know about other people and how you can help your fellow brother. Asking curious questions is the best way to get there.

You should also be curious about asking questions about your business. You do not have to reinvent the wheel because the answer is probably out there. Become more curious about growing your business by asking others how they do it.

- Ask yourself why you do things the way you do them now.
- Who does it differently? Most businesspeople want to talk to their competitors. I learned from some commercial real estate agents that they did this because one might have the buyer and another agent might have the seller. So, they stay in touch. I now stay in touch with other mortgage professionals because I might be able to do a loan they can't do.
- How do other companies differ from how mine does things? I like to ask other businesspeople how they market their attorney practice or plumbing business. They might be doing something I haven't thought of. When I realized how effective it was for real estate agents to send out a monthly marketing newsletter, I got curious about it and started putting together one for my business. Today, it is the heart of my business.
- Is your product or service what the marketplace wants? Contact others to see who is doing really well and who is not. Most of the time, the folks doing well have focused on a niche you may want to consider.
- Be curious about your BUZZ. "Are people talking about me the way I want them to?" Start asking others what folks are saying about you on the street.
- Have you asked your employees curious questions? Are they doing what they want to do? Do they feel like they have ownership and a deep understanding of what you are trying to accomplish? Most employees want to get better at their craft and want to be involved with *their* cause, not yours!

Create Your Own Club

A lot of my friends tell me they don't like the groups that are already out there for them to join. Maybe they're not focused on what they feel is important. So, create your own club. Here are some examples:

Breakfast Club

I noticed that the old men at the local restaurant had a table they sat around, bull-shitting all morning. The problem was they were older and were not interested in doing business. They were all retired. So, I created my own breakfast club. I invited some friends to come, and before long, we had five to ten people showing up every Tuesday at the local restaurant to talk about things important to us.

After a while, I ran into a guy who managed a Waffle House and asked him to join our group. After a time or two, he said "Why don't we do this at the Waffle House?"

So, the next week we went, and boy, did he hook us up. He had a table with a white tablecloth and flowers on it, and we even had our own server. You should have seen the look on people's faces when they came in and saw us sitting at what looked like the king's table. He even got us Waffle House shirts and hats. We did that for several years and I got a lot of business out of it. We all invited anyone we knew, and the group was always changing.

Bible Study

This one is easy because there are a lot of them in my area, but mostly people get their own group because they want to make sure they are sharing with like-minded people.

Lunch

I have done several of these at different restaurants. Usually, it starts with a new restaurant that needs to generate business. I told them I would help by getting the word out to my buddies that, every Thursday, we would meet at this restaurant. I would focus mainly on new people I had just met and wanted to build a better, deeper relationship with. I always told them to come because I could introduce them to new people they could do business with—and they did.

Investor Club

Recently, a few guys suggested we start a club to find ways to invest in real estate in the area. We decided to add bourbon tasting to the event. Next thing I knew, we had eight people show up. I invited four and another friend who brought up the idea invited four. We decided to meet every other month so we'll see how it goes. But in the meantime, I met four new people and one has already started referring business to me.

Whiskey or Wine Club

Doug Haney invites his friends over for whiskey tasting. Each person brings a bottle of bourbon then draws a number. The person who draws the lowest number gets to choose which bottle he or she can take home.

Doggy Playdate Club

Contact all of your dog-owner friends and designate one day a week for play dates with their dogs. It could be at someone's house or the local dog park.

Motorcycle Club

Get all your motorhead friends together for a weekend ride. Could be once a month or quarterly.

Home Tours Club

Go to an older town and tour antebellum homes and have lunch with the group afterward. Find out who in your network has a passion for architecture and history.

Outside Looking In

Are you on the outside looking in?

I had worked at the largest traditional clothing store in Atlanta for several years and thought I was ready to do my own thing. After a couple of slow months of business, my dad—who was my investor—thought it would be a good idea to hire a consultant. We needed to get the party started!

A lot of times we were inside our business, looking out to the sidewalk, saying, "Why aren't those people coming in to see me? Why aren't they coming into my building or shopping center?"

The consultant told me I was looking at it all wrong. He said, "You need to be on the outside, looking in." So, we went out in the parking lot of my clothing store, and stood in the parking lot. He asked me a few questions. "Why would I want to come into your store?" "Is there anything in the window that entices me to come in?" "Is there a sign?" "Is there any reason that says I need to go in there and see what all this is about?"

There wasn't! I often think about that, even in the mortgage and speaking business.

I have to *give* you a reason to come in and see me. That's not just a retail thing. If you're a real estate agent, does your sign say, "Come in and look at my listing?" You must think about the advertising you're doing because a lot of times we're just stuck inside too much.

Are you out there trying to figure out why people would want to come see you? Why they would want to call you? Why they would want to visit your webpage? Spend some time today thinking about what makes people want to call you. "What do I have? What's different about me? What's unique, what's special?" Understand we are all special in our own unique way and you need to be vulnerable in letting people know that. There is something special about you. It's your job to figure out what's special about you so people will spend money with you.

THE CLOTHES HORSE—Charleen has a men's clothing store. The space is unique. A small entrance and only one window to look in. Once inside, the space is small. Charleen knew if she could get people to come inside, she would sell more stuff, but people just walked by.

So, she got creative.

She started bringing her store out on the sidewalk, displaying her goods so people would know what was inside. Then she came up with the idea to have a musician perform right in front of the store on the sidewalk. That worked too. Now she's worked out a deal with the bar next door to do tastings of wine and special liquor drinks in the very back of the store. She greets folks on the street and offers them a cocktail for free in the back of the store. Because she was on the outside looking in, she has found several ways to get people into her store and sales are booming.

Google Reviews/ Testimonials

When my son Connor got into the mortgage business with me, he was looking for a way to increase our online business. He wanted to try all sorts of things, but I was reluctant to buy leads and pay-per-click advertising. After getting feedback from other businesspeople, he realized we needed to have more reviews and testimonials on Google. He came up with the idea to send every past client a link to rate us on Google. The rankings all came in at five stars. Next thing we knew, the phone calls started coming in from people who saw we had positive comments on Google. Now we send every customer a Google link to rate us. It probably gets us one extra deal a month, minimum.

Referrals

This whole book is about getting more referrals.
Here are some rules I follow:

- If you refer to someone and they don't refer you back, *fire them*!

I remember when I changed from my family dentist to a friend I went to high school with. He was new in his practice, and I wanted to help him succeed. One day, while in the chair, he mentioned he had bought a new house. I asked him who he used for his loan, and he said the bank.

I said, "You know, I'm in the mortgage business, why didn't you give me a call?"

He said, "I just didn't think about it."

The agent gave him a lender and he just went with it. I told him it broke my heart that I was spending money with him and he never gave me a chance. On that day, everything I thought about referrals changed. I fired him!

"I'm going to find me another dentist," I told him, "because the dentist I want to use will send me business and I will send them business."

He looked at me with a quizzical look. Some people just don't get it. They are takers not givers!

Then, I went to another guy I went to high school with who was a dentist. I told him the story about our other friend and why I fired him. I told him he could be my dentist if he referred me customers. But better than that, I will send him more customers than he sends me. You see, I do loans for people who are new or just moving to this area, they will need a dentist. He said okay, but I wasn't sure he understood.

Then one day, I was in for a cleaning and when he came to

check my teeth, he said, "Sally, did you tell Steve about your new house?"

I said, "No, she didn't."

She went on to explain that she had bought a new house and then I asked her who she used for her mortgage. She used someone the agent referred her to. I asked if he was a customer and she said no. I said, "Bob, you remember I told you I was only going to stay your customer as long as we referred each other business or at least give each other a shot?"

He said, "Yeah, I should have told her to call you."

That's when I got up and walked away. I walked out right in the middle of the cleaning. I see him all around town and to this day he doesn't get it. Nice people, a great dentist, but I don't do that kind of business anymore. I would rather say I don't have a referral for you than to send it to someone else who won't reciprocate. Done with it.

As I was looking for a new dentist, the dentist who was in my Rotary Club called me about a loan and I *knew* who my new dentist was going to be. He sends me personal referrals and I do the same for him. Guess what? He is the most expensive guy in town, but he is good at his craft. He returns my calls on the weekend when my daughter's tooth is aching and I take his call on the weekends when he is looking for a new property.

Sometimes people screw up. Recently my main insurance referral guy told me he was moving to another town to take over a great opportunity. He wanted to know if I would still keep my insurance with him and I said I would. We had built a great relationship and so there was no reason it couldn't continue. Then, the next time I saw him, he mentioned he was buying a new house and I realized I was not his lender. After a day or so of thinking about it, I called him and told him I was disappointed. I thought *I was his mortgage guy*, and I didn't understand why I wasn't doing his loan. He started explaining it to me and I said it didn't matter because I never even got a chance to compete for his business or be consulted about the deal. I asked him to think about it overnight and call me the next day.

When he called back, he apologized and said he really screwed up. He swore it wouldn't happen again and wanted to continue doing business. I'll stay with him because I believe he did screw up and that he is truly sorry. I think we can keep growing our businesses together.

So, sometimes you can forgive, but you have to let them know how you feel.

- Look for people who get the referral game.

If you do, you will light each other up and grow your network. My best agents refer me business and I refer them business. I go out of my way to find them customers (or husbands). I feel like a failure if I don't send you any business and you have sent business my way. The weight of reciprocity is strong in me and I would rather be one up on you than you one up on me.

- Understand everyone's sweet spot.

Know who is a perfect customer for them. If you hate to cold call, use this as a way to touch base with people and ask them, "What is the perfect customer I can send you?"

- Fire the cheapo referrals.

Some of the customers you gave a deal to are cheap and you let them whittle you down. Now everyone they send you is the same way. "Call Beech, he will do it for next to nothing." Fire these people. Tell them you did them a favor but you're pretty damn good at what you do and you need them to refer you people based on your skills, not your price.

Are You Good Enough?

One of the most limiting beliefs we have is "Are you good enough?" If you believe you are good at what you do, then the way you approach your work is totally different than if you question your abilities.

The first thing you need to do is have product knowledge. If you have product knowledge, you feel better about the discussion you have with potential customers. The best way to get better product knowledge is to take one area you are weak in and get a mentor to help you in that area. If you are an insurance agent and you feel weak in life insurance, then go find someone who is really good at life insurance and ask them to apprentice you. Spend some time in their office or take them to lunch. Ask a lot of questions and learn from the king.

Second thing is my theory called "360." Think about all the people who touch your business and go see them. For instance, if you are a mortgage or banking professional, you deal with real estate closing attorneys. Learn as much as you can about what they do. Spend time with them learning the ins and outs of their trade. Do the same thing with your appraiser, surveyors, and real estate agents.

If you do these two things, you will feel smarter, more confident, and more knowledgeable. And, you will have developed a relationship with people you can call on for questions.

You want to be the guy who has the answer or knows who has the answer. So many people in your profession don't have this desire to be better at what they do. They just go through the motions.

When you feel you are good enough, then it comes across to

your customers as trustworthy and professional. They will feel better about spending money with you.

Remember the objective is to be constantly learning. Be the person who spends money on yourself and has a desire to go to conferences and read more about what you do. Once you feel good enough, you will then challenge your customers to see your way of thinking because you can back it up with expertise and knowledge that the other salesperson/owner doesn't have.

Are you good enough? [1]

---

[1] Steve Beecham, "Are You Good Enough," video.stevebeecham.com, accessed September 28, 2023, https://video.stevebeecham.com/media/motivational-speaking-speaking-promo-videos-are-you-good-enough-324274.

Circle the Wagons

Is there somebody you want to meet? Maybe you want to talk to them about a job, or you want to talk to them about business. Basically, they are a PROSPECT.

You have two options for meeting them: warm or cold.

Cold is what we call "cold calling." You just go to their office or walk up to them and introduce yourself. They have no idea who you are, and they might think you're weird. Most people hate this method, but it is better than not taking the chance.

Or, you can get a "warm" introduction. This means someone introduces you to them. It is the best way to meet someone.

Think back to your dating days. If you had to rely on meeting someone at a bar you didn't know, that was tough. But if you had a mutual friend the introduction was easy.

I call that "Circling the Wagons."

Circling the Wagons is like cowboys and Indians. Cowboys used to get their wagons and circle them up around the campfire. The Indians would ride around the wagons shooting arrows into the wagons, but the circle protected the cowboys in the middle. Pretend your prospect is right in the middle of the wagons sitting by the campfire, and you want to meet as many people around that person (the wagon people) as you can. You are trying to get a warm introduction to the person sitting at the campfire. The more people you can get to introduce you to that person, the better chance you have of doing business with them.

You just never know who they know. Chances are there are some people who know both of you and your goal is to get them to introduce you. That's where you get creative.

The best thing to do is to be like an FBI agent. Go on Facebook,

A FEW BIG IDEAS

LinkedIn, and Instagram and try to find out who their friends are. Then call them and ask, "Hey, could you introduce me to this person sitting at the campfire?" Chances are a lot of those folks will do it. That way, when you get to that person, you both have a mutual connection. Because you have people in common and those people mentioned you, there's a really good chance they'll meet with you.

People think, "If I hear your name once that is just OK. If I hear your name a second time, I know you must be IMPORTANT!"

I have a podcast I do once a month on Spotify and iTunes (Beech Talks). I thought it would be cool to get Herschel Walker—Heisman Trophy-winning University of Georgia running back, who decided to run for the United States senate for Georgia—on the podcast so I set out to make that happen by using the Circle the Wagons theory. The first person I contacted was Frank Ros. Frank was the captain of Herschel's 1980 national champions team and a very close friend to Herschel. I met Frank because his wife and my wife went to high school together. I contacted Frank about having Herschel on the podcast and he said he would talk to Herschel about it. In the meantime, I mentioned it to my son Connor. Connor let me know that a friend of his was working on Herschel's campaign and that her family lived in Alpharetta near me. I asked Connor to reach out to her about asking him to appear on the podcast. About that time, another friend called me and asked me to come to a fundraiser for Herschel he was having at his house.

I then told Frank I would be seeing Herschel and Frank called him and told him we were friends. When Mary and I met Herschel, we talked about our common friends and I mentioned I would like to have him on the podcast. Several months later, the campaign agreed to give me a thirty-minute interview.

Own Your Own Backyard

For years I was in a group called Vistage.
Vistage is an organization for business owners and their key employees. We meet every month and at a lot of meetings, we had speakers. One day, we had this speaker introduced to us by our leader. This older gentleman walked into the room. He was in his late seventies or early eighties. He asked us to guess what he used to do for a living. After a few minutes, and no one guessing correctly, he said he helped invent Ronald McDonald and the Quarter Pounder with Cheese. They ended up with one of the most famous advertising campaigns ever. He was the retired head of marketing for McDonald's.

He talked about the success they had and how people were lined up to buy franchises but had no hamburger experience. They decided to not let people buy another franchise until they owned a hamburger business within a three-mile radius of their current location. "After all," he said, "we were in the hamburger and milkshake business."

You have to own the area around you first. Your own neighborhood. So many people get caught up in getting customers in the next town or county. Before you do that, you need to be the mayor of your own town.

The milkman and the garbage company all know this. These companies that run routes want to add a new truck and route, but not until they know they can own the area. It doesn't make economic sense to expand and add a route on the west side of town because your truck needs to be there all day, not half a day.

Routes have to be set up in close proximity. My friend Mobil Joe, who is in the grass-cutting business, will grow his business and then come back and fire some customers because they are not strategically located. "If I can pull my truck up and knock out three to five lawns without putting the equipment back on the truck, that's utopia!" says Mobil Joe.

Fortune 500 companies *cannot* compete with you in hand-to-hand combat. The closer you are to the customer, the less others can take them away from you. Why? Because they can see and touch them, and they know where you live.

I do not have a car salesman at the local GMC dealer. The reason why is all the people that work there are not from my town. Now, all the service guys are local. Doug and Steve live in the community and are part of Rotary and coach Little League ball. But the sales guys are not from around here. No one goes in and buys a car because they know the sales guy from the PTA. All their business is price oriented and most of it is on the internet and they never build relationships with the community. The service department, on the other hand, is the best-performing piece of their business. Local!

Two of my uncles used to own Waffle House restaurants. One of them told me that one of the best marketing campaigns they have ever done is to convince the store manager to stop at a business on the way to work and on the way home. They were to just pick a random business, walk in, and introduce themselves as the local manager, and ask the receptionist what their favorite food was at Waffle House. Then, they would get their business card out and write on the back, "Free omelet-pecan waffle, T-bone steak for Jane." Then ask them to come say hello when they come in because they'd probably be there since they are open 24/7.

This one idea was huge for Waffle House as they started to realize that local business was the best and most reliable business they could have. Before that, they always thought it was highway traffic business, but came to realize the local person might eat there five days a week.

What are some things you can do to promote yourself as the local person or mayor of your village?

Meet the local public safety chief and ask him to bring a fire truck or police car to a neighborhood for the kids to see. Better yet, have them come by for a six-year-old birthday party. They love to do this!

Politicians need to meet as many people as they can. Walk the neighborhood with someone running for public office. Throw a party at your office or house and invite your friends.

Fortune 500 company marketing executives want to know how to meet people 'under the water tower' in every town. They want to get as close to the local people as they can. That's why Coke used to sponsor scoreboards at Little League fields. But, you have a leg up on them. You know the people at these places and can get in there faster and cheaper, so put your name on the concession stand.

Start by owning your street! Then start owning your neighborhood, then businesses within walking distance of your home and office. That's what real estate agents call farming. They pick the closest neighborhoods they want to do business in and then they start mailing everyone and letting them know what's going on and how much they know the area.

You can do that too!

Spoke and Hub

This is a little trick I learned when I had my clothing store. My consultant taught me this particular technique and I think it's one of the best ways to increase your business with very little effort. I call it "Spoke and Hub."

I live in Atlanta and we have this interstate highway called I-285 that goes around Atlanta. And, then we have this state highway called 400 that goes north. My business location is right there. And so, this consultant said to me, "Steve, what if somebody doesn't buy from you, where do they go?"

And I said, "Well, they go buy at the mall."

He said, "Okay, are there other people that have little clothing stores like yours?"

And I said, "Yeah, there's one over there. There's one over there. There's one over there. There's one up there. And there's one down there."

He said, "Well, what do they carry differently from you?"

And I said, "Well, it's all about the same. Some have a little more expensive stuff. Some have a little less expensive stuff. They carry some different lines."

He said, "So here's what I want you to do. I want you to go to each one of those clothing stores, and I want you to say to them, if I have a customer and that customer needs a navy blazer, and I don't have the right size or the right price, can I call you? And if you've got what my customer is looking for, will you sell it to him? Or will you let me buy it from you at your price and resell it to him? Or if you won't steal him, I'll send him to see you. Because he may need it for that evening or something." Then he said, "You'll find that every one of these people will participate with you in that."

I went to these people and I spoke to each one of them. I said, "Hey, if you'll work with me on this, I can send you extra customers." They all said yes. And what I found out is we all thought we were competitors with each other. However, I became the hub and they were the spokes.

I became the go-to guy for them. I was the one who broke the ice in our relationship. Every Saturday I'd have a lot of business. If I didn't have something a customer wanted, I would call one of these people and send my customer over there or I'd send somebody to run out there and pick it up and bring it back for them.

An amazing thing happened. My business increased 20 percent. What happened was I was sending to each one maybe one sale a month. But every one of them was sending me one customer a month. Because I took the initiative to go meet them, I received more business than them.

Maybe you're a financial advisor and there are certain things you're really smart about, but there are certain things you really don't know much about. Maybe it's better for you to send your customer to somebody else, maybe in a different state or in a different town. But think about who you can talk to that would be a great referral source for you because they do something you don't, or they have some inventory you don't have. Create a little Spoke and Hub situation and you'll find that your business will increase 10 to 20 percent.

One year, I was at a convention. One of the things I wanted to accomplish was meeting someone from Arkansas. The reason was I love to duck hunt and I had two little boys I wanted to take duck hunting. The problem was I needed a farmer who would let me bring them and not be concerned about the hunting so much as my boys having fun. That way if it was too cold or wet they could go back to the farmhouse.

As I walked down the hall, I passed a guy with Jonesboro, Arkansas, on his badge. I grabbed him and hugged him and told him he was my new best friend. He was startled and taken back and thought I was crazy! I told him my desire and he said he had an uncle who had a farm that fit the bill. We called the uncle and his son that day and for the next seven or so years, I hunted with this fine family. We hunted as if we were family and my boys loved it.

But the real story was that it was so easy to make that happen. I then realized I needed to meet other people from other states I could build relationships with. I had a lot of customers buying second homes in Florida, so I set out to meet someone from the panhandle of Florida. I set out to meet someone near Hilton Head. I set out to meet someone from Colorado. These were all states I could refer my customers to. Everyone was glad to meet me when I told them I wanted to send them customers. I mentioned if they ever had someone moving to Georgia, I would love to help.

We would not exchange any money, just me sending you business and you sending me business. Still to this day, I have people calling me from other states with referrals and I do the same. This is business I never would have received and vice versa. I know real estate agents do this a good bit, especially if they are with a national company, but you can do it in your business too. Set a goal to meet others like you in all fifty states. Be the Hub and let them be your Spokes.

Buying Leads

Don't do it!
It's a cop-out!

A lot of people start out buying leads because it can be a faster way to get your business going. It is expensive, but you can make it work for you if you do this one important thing. Save every email from everyone you talk to and put it in your database. If you do that and call them every year, you can build a database from scratch. Buying leads should just be a way to get going until your other marketing habits start paying off.

There are different kinds of leads, but the ones I would focus on are the ones that give you a volume of people to work on over the next couple of years. Basically, you are buying emails and cell-phone numbers. Most people buy something we are selling every three to seven years. If you do not get a deal off the lead, please keep the email and call on a regular basis and you will not throw that money away.

If you do the other stuff I mention in this book, like joining organizations and working your village, you will not need to buy leads. Most people who buy leads get in the habit of doing that and not being very social, so they get stuck calling leads and paying for them. No highly successful person selling is still buying leads!

In the real estate business, it is common for agents to buy leads. Companies like Zillow and Realtor.com have their inside sales reps calling agents all day persuading them to buy zip codes. While you can get leads from these sources, the return on investment is usually not worth it. Most of the leads are people who are kicking tires online. A lot of them are not qualified to buy a home and some never will be.

Some of the lead-provider companies have started offering leads in exchange for a referral fee. This is a much better type of program than writing a check for hundreds or thousands of dollars to buy a zip code.

Again, if you choose this route, ensure you are following up with each and every lead. This is not the way you want to build your business in the long term.

This is a short-term solution only.

The Tapes You Play in Your Head

The tapes you play in your head, the things you tell yourself, are the biggest single thing I've ever learned. How you talk to yourself is what kind of person you become. And I think if you have to think about that, there's not always good thoughts in your head.

I read a great book by Napoleon Hill called *Outwitting the Devil*. Hill also wrote the book *Think and Grow Rich*.

After he wrote the book and went out on the speaking tour, he realized they would walk away from his speeches motivated. And then three days, four days, or weeks later, the motivation went away. He kept wondering, *How can I keep people fired up?* or *How can I get them to change their thoughts?* or *Can I get them to change their habits?*

One of the stories I talk about when I speak is about Napoleon Hill having a crisis and ending up scared for his life and isolating in a cabin in West Virginia. While he was there, he had a lot of time to think.

One of the things he thought about was how to get people to understand the fear he felt. He came up with this idea for a book and he wrote *Outwitting the Devil*. It's about having a conversation with the devil. He would say to the devil, "How come you put fear in me about going and knocking on that guy's door and going in there and asking him for business?"

The devil responded, "That's my job." And he was winning 95 percent of the time. The devil's job is to put those negative thoughts into your head.

And so, through this book, Napoleon was trying to make the point that you have negative thoughts and you have positive thoughts. But, you have a lot more negative thoughts than you have positive thoughts—making it so much easier to have negative thoughts.

After reading the book, I was thinking, *How do I explain this to people when I'm speaking on stage?* So I came up with this visual. You hold your hand up and you make a "hook 'em" horns like the Texas Longhorns fans do. Then you take the two middle fingers and move them against the thumb—that's the devil talking. Pretend that's the devil talking to you: your product costs too much, you're not dressed properly, and nobody wants to buy from you because they already have someone they love.

But then you can take your other hand and you make a circle like the halo of an angel. And these are the angel's wings. The angel can talk to you too, just like the devil can talk to you.

So when the devil says, "No, they don't want to talk to you."

The angel says, "Oh, you're awesome, Steve. You've always been one of the top salespeople at your company. Your grandmother loves you." You can say whatever you want.

When I realized I heard the devil talk to me, I looked at him and said, "Don't talk to me like that. I don't want to hear it."

I then look at the angel, and she says, "Hey man, you're a rock star. You can do this."

And so, I want to challenge you. When you hear these negative thoughts, how can you put in a positive thought? How can you bring in something to knock out the negative?

I went on a trip with some very successful people. Long story short, we were flying on their private jet and I said to one of them, "Andy, what are the tapes you play in your head?"

He said, "What do you mean, Beech?"

I said, "What do you say to yourself when something's not going right?"

And he said, "Oh yeah, I always tell myself, I'm the luckiest guy."

I asked, "How many times a day do you tell yourself that you're the luckiest guy in the world?"

He answered, "I don't know, a couple hundred.

And I went, "Oh my gosh."

Another guy was sitting there on the plane; another wealthy individual. I said, "Mike, what do you say to yourself?"

He said, "I can do it better than you."

I said, "Really?"

He said, "Yeah, through a series of events in my life, I got into things and figured them out better than other people. I had more desire. I came up with the ideas and every time I look at a business, I can figure out how I can do it better than you."

I asked, "How many times do you say that at night?"

He answered, "Every time I look at a business, I say that. I'd drive down the road in our hometown. And I think about that business or that business. I do this forty, fifty times on the way to work."

I thought, *I'm not thinking like that.*

And then I went out and spent some time with a guy I went to high school with. He ended up being a Major League Baseball player and got a World Series ring (and played in two World Series). His name is Tony Phillips. You may know him. He played for the Oakland A's and Detroit Tigers. Tony and I went to high school together and I hadn't seen him since. I ended up on a speaking engagement out in Phoenix, where he lives now. Prior to that, about six months earlier, he had come to town to go to a mutual friend's daughter's wedding, and when he came to town, I picked him up at my friend's house. I drove him around that weekend because he didn't rent a car, so he and I got to spend some time together and talk.

Later, when I went to Phoenix, I called him and said, "Hey, I'll be in Phoenix. Let's meet for dinner one night."

And he said, "No, your butt's mine."

I said, "What do you mean?"

He said, "You picked me up. You took me everywhere I needed to be when I was in town, we'll do the same thing for you."

And I said, "No, you really don't need to."

He said, "I have nothing to do, I'm retired."

Once he picked me up at the airport, I said, "Tony, tell me about what's going on. What are you doing for business?"

He answered, "Well, I've invested in this baseball, Beech, it has numbers on it. So that when you throw it to a kid, you'd say, catch the number one. And when you throw it to them, they're looking for number one. They really can't see it, but it makes them focus on the ball."

I said, "Really? What are you going to do with that?"

He said, "Well, I'm going to sell it. I'm going to make millions on it. It's going to be great for the kids to learn how to hit. Beech, my shit always works out."

I came back to Atlanta and as I was doing loans, I was talking to people about speaking engagements. I would say to myself, "I'm the luckiest guy in the world. My shit always works out. I know how to do it better than anybody else." And I started changing my thought process.

I want you to think about that. I want you to realize that highly successful people talk to themselves differently than people who aren't highly successful.

I had an opportunity to go to breakfast one morning and sat beside Evander Holyfield. And I asked him, "Evander, what's the tape you play in your head, man?"

He didn't want to quit talking about it. He had two or three tapes through different periods of his life. Things that had happened that changed his focus, changed the way he thought about things.

I'm telling you all these people who are highly successful are playing extremely positive tapes in their heads. And they're saying it multiple times a day. If you want to change where you're going, you have to change the tape. You can't let the devil talk to you anymore. You need to talk to the angels. So change the tape that you're playing in your head.

Three Things Expert Salespeople Do

I got a call from a friend of mine one day. He said, "Beech, I am kind of struggling in my business. I need to go to the next level. I am doing well, but I want to do better and be an expert at what I do."

There are *three things I think experts do better than anybody else:*

1. Paint a better picture to the person in front of you, of what it is you are looking for. If I am sitting there and talking to you, I need to leave you with a picture. I want to put you in a movie so when you see what I described, then you are really clear to get the right person in touch with me.

2. The internal conversation you are having with yourself is key. High achievers are talking to themselves differently than you are. Your current internal conversation has gotten you to the level you are at now, but to get to the next level, you have to change that conversation you're having with yourself. It has to be forward-thinking. It has to be more positive. It has to be, "Hey, I am going after it and I know I can do it."

3. One of my favorites, especially for people who do not have a sales manager, is to create a list of the top 100 people you would like to meet in a year who could change your life.

Now, the list is not always prospects. The list is comprised of people in the community, people you can get to because you want to meet them and learn from them or about their business. Some of them will be able to introduce you to people who will move you along in your journey. But the whole objective is to create a prospective list of really cool people. You go out and meet those people because you are curious about them. They are not all potential customers. It may be your mayor, your state representative, or your kid's school teacher. It might be a business you ride by every day and you're wondering what's going on inside! It might be somebody you know about in your community who has been successful, and you would just like to meet them.

All successful salespeople we know do these three things. They make it clear who they want to do business with. They are humble narcissists. They constantly work on expanding their network.

Work on these three things and you will go to the next level!

Time Management

A lot of us have problems with time management, especially if you're in sales. So, here are three things you can do to improve your time management:

1. Turn off the notifications you're receiving on your cell phone. If you receive notifications for Facebook and Instagram turn those notifications off. You may want to leave your phone or your texts on so you can check those occasionally. The more of those you turn off, the more time you'll have for yourself. If you get distracted like Mark and I, this is a must!

2. You need to schedule appointments with yourself. If you had a doctor's appointment, you will be unavailable during that hour. Put in a time slot with your name on it each day you're going to spend time doing what it is you need to do to make your business better.

3. You need to figure out how you can block a period of time out every day for thirty minutes. In those thirty minutes, don't return any phone calls, don't look at any emails. For the next thirty minutes, focus on getting done what you need to get done. Put your phone in the bathroom for thirty minutes and leave your computer desk. Take a pad and paper with you so you have no distractions.

Remember that you are the one responsible for your time management. Try those. See if they won't help you with your time management.

Another important time management idea is managing your workday. I worked at Wendy's when I was sixteen. I realized it was a manufacturing process. The order was taken, then someone made the fries, drinks, and hamburgers that ended up at the other end of the counter in a bag. It was just an assembly line process.

When I got into the mortgage business, I realized it was the same thing. You call about a loan and then we get an appraisal done, lock your loan, get a loan application taken, and end up at the closing attorney's office. So how do you manage that manufacturing process?

In the mortgage business, you have deadlines. You have very angry people if they have booked a moving truck and they can't move that day. You have an angry real estate agent if she is not going to pick up her check that day. Closing on time is a big deal. So, I instituted an idea called the Fire Drill.

Fire Drill means that when you start working on a loan you go to your calendar and put the dates certain task items need to be done.

If it is not done, then you have a FIRE—one that needs to be put out *that day* and *at that moment*. This keeps the manufacturing line open to a smooth closing.

As I have taught this to others, I have begun to realize that almost all businesses can institute the Fire Drill. We all have a system that starts with the conversation with the customer and ends up with the product or service being delivered. Think about the disasters you have had in your business and institute a way to avoid them by being proactive with reminders on your calendar. Also, share these fire dates with your staff so everyone is working toward the same goal.

Real estate agents have deadlines also after writing a contract. When is the earnest money due? When is the due diligence or appraisal period ending? All of these dates should be on your calendar.

If you truly want to run a successful business, then you must have your prospecting time on your calendar. Block out an hour a day for prospecting and lead follow-up activities. Block out more time for having lunch or coffee with your A-list referral sources or past clients. On Monday morning or Sunday night, look at your calendar for the week and ensure these activities are on your schedule.

Entrepreneurship

Entrepreneurs run a business. They are not technicians or just salespeople, they are in charge of making sure all the pieces run smoothly.

Think about the pieces like majors in business school. Most of us are just salespeople who wanted to work for ourselves and not have someone looking over our shoulder. We wanted the freedom of doing it our way. The question is, have you just created a sales job or a small business? You can't have a business to be happy or to have time with your kids as the sole purpose. These are not "changing the world" goals, so the chance of success is limited because there isn't a world-changing reason.

Here are some examples of how your business might break down:

Accounting

This could be run with QuickBooks. This is balancing your checkbook. You need to set up an account for your business and run it that way. You need a monthly profit/loss statement so you can look at what you're actually making each month. You also need to do projections on what you will do and balance that out based on slow times and busy times.

Make sure you are taking full advantage of all tax deductions by hiring a CPA. For instance, you and a friend decide to start a business together. One way to keep it nice and clean is to get a credit card you use strictly for the business and a company checking account. You can also get a company car and have the business pay all the expenses of the car. If the company needs money, you make a stockholder loan to the company and then when you have cash, you pay yourself back. You can also have the company give you a W2 and you can set up a payroll company or do it in QuickBooks to pay yourself and any employees.

Advertising

This is different than marketing. This is actually understanding how to lay out or place an ad. This is your logo and business card. This is the sign on your car door or window.

This would include your newsletter layout and templates. Also, what about your social media strategy? Which sites and who is your target market?

Management

Do you show up for work? Do you manage your workflow on a timely basis? Do you show up for appointments? Do you have the marketing material ready for your listing presentation? Is there a work/life balance?

Do an organizational chart for yourself and your employees. Talk about where they bring the most value to the company. Circle the place you are best and talk about getting others to do the other parts you are not good at or do not desire doing.

Economics

What is the local economy doing? Is it headed for a recession? Look at factors such as employment and cost of living. Are housing prices going up or down?

Are you prepared for an increase in business? Do you need to hire more employees?

Finance

This is about knowing how to predict the future and getting money to do that. This is understanding that if you want to bring someone on as an assistant, you will be slower in productivity as you are training them and getting them ramped up. You might need to get a line of credit to help you do this. You may need it to do an advertising campaign and borrow from your line of credit.

Bootstrapping means starting a business with little or no money. You don't *borrow* money. Borrowing money is not a good thing to do, especially when it comes to using it on advertising. You are better off finding ways to market that don't cost you anything. It is slower to grow but when you spend your hard-earned cash, you are more careful.

Human Resources

Do I hire an assistant? Do I have a way to list out what I need them to do and to make sure they are qualified? Have I given them a list of things they need to do for me each day, week, or month? Are they clear on what can get them fired or get them promoted? Have I set up a plan for them to grow with my organization? Are employees clear on what expectations are? Do they have benefits? A great book on this subject is *Mentored by a Millionaire* by Steve Scott.

Marketing

Knowing where and how to promote the company is important. Do I go to chamber meetings or buy Facebook ads? How much money do I spend on Zillow ads or how many expired listings do I call each day? Do I take cookies to the neighbors or put an ad in the school bulletin? The question is, do I put a budget together with finance and advertising to have a consistent program?

Public Relations

Buzz! Am I getting quoted in local newspapers and blogs? Do I have a brand that is special and unique? Am I showing up at functions where my buyers are and promoting my company? How about bad PR or bad Buzz that's out there? Am I spinning it to help my company?

Law

Not a business degree but we sure need an understanding of this since we are doing contracts for a living. You need a good attorney to help with writing contracts for vendors and employees. You may need help collecting payment for invoices.

There also has to be a very clear vision from you of where you are going that is understood by your employees and customers. But it needs to be CRYSTAL CLEAR with you.

Vision is the hallmark of a great entrepreneur!

Entrepreneurs find a *niche*. This might be something brand new or something just a little different. Most people just find a better way to do something that already exists and don't come up with a totally brand-new idea. Elon Musk with Tesla is a great example. He didn't invent the car or the battery.

Your niche should become the core focus of what you do every day. It is your voice to the outside world. What is your calling to others?

You Can't Grow If You Don't Let Go

The people who have the biggest problem with this concept are usually very successful. Very successful people do not delegate very well—they have to learn to let go. They are not the top 1 percent but the rest of us 99 percenters. In order to get to the top 1 percent, you have to let go!

When coaching or consulting with successful businesspeople, I see people just can't let go of certain things. There are typically three areas of letting go.

1. Letting go of day-to-day tasks. Being better at delegation.
2. Letting go of certain customers.
3. Letting go of time killers to give you time to think and strategize about the business.

If you owned a restaurant and you tried to do everything, you're not going to be very successful. You can't wash the dishes, cook the food, serve the customers, clean up and write checks at the end of the day, and still run a great business. You have to start letting go. So, you have to start looking around at some of the things you're doing and figuring out who you can delegate to. You have to let go of certain tasks. If you don't, your mind can't have time to think about ways to improve your business.

Michael Gerber wrote a great book on this titled *The E-Myth* (see chapter "Hiring" for the *E-Myth* pyramid). It is a must-read for any small-business person starting a business. The main takeaway for me was getting you to draw an organizational chart. This chart changed everything for me.

On the first chart I filled out, I was everything. CEO, CFO, CIO, sales manager, marketer, and clean-up crew. Gerber gets you to draw a chart based on where you want the company to ultimately be in five, ten, and twenty years.

When you start, every box in the organization may have your name on it or, in my case, one box had my wife's name on it (bookkeeper). Then you figure out what box you could fill with someone else to give you the most time to increase the business. Then do the next one and the next one.

Eventually, you have a chart at the end that says, "THIS IS MY BEST BOX. This is where I bring the most value to the enterprise." That's the box you want to end up in. As time goes on, you eventually let go of the boxes to others so you can grow!

Next is to let go of some customers. Yep, fire the bottom 20 percent who you don't make any money with and the complainers who suck up your time.

Mark has a cancellation guarantee for all his clients. He does not lock them into a listing or buyer brokerage agreement. State law says we have to have an agreement in place so he has everyone sign the agreement. But his clients can fire him for any reason AND he can fire them also. The reason for this is that there are a lot of people who will not follow his advice and then blame him for their house not selling. Or they are unreasonable about certain activities. If there is a client who would never agree to show the home, he would have a conversation about the importance of showings. If the client still did not change, he would part ways with them in a very nice way.

I once heard a guy say all he did was look to buy companies he could go in and fire the bottom 20 percent of the customers and raise the price by 20 percent. He laid out a formula he used for raising prices and giving better customer service. He said life was more fun and he made a lot more money with less headache. I adopted that formula, and it is so true. Let go of the losers.

My CPA told me he can't bring himself to let go the little old ladies and the folks who got him started. But they are not profitable and it's not where, in my opinion, he can make the most money and have a better work-life balance. He won't do it, so what happens is he is running off some profitable customers because they feel like he doesn't have the time for them.

My suggestion to him was to bring in a younger associate and let him take care of the bottom 20 percent. A lot of companies do that in financial and insurance services. They bring in a new guy and let him work out of a top producer's office and then the top producer gives him the bottom 20 percent of his business to seed the new guy and to give the pro more time to get other big hitters.

The third thing is time to reflect. We get into a routine of doing certain things and we don't let stuff go. Because we are just *busy*, we can't spend time on how to expand our business. Think about the things you can let go of today. What can you delegate to someone? What should you not be doing anymore? It's amazing how many things you can get rid of if you really want to. You need to give yourself time at the beginning of the day, the middle of the day, the end of the day, or on the weekends to think about how you can grow your business. You need some free-thinking time. And the only way you get that is by letting go of certain responsibilities. Plus, it's a bonus to the person you are delegating as they always want more responsibility.

You have to let go. If you don't let go, then your mind won't have time to think about ways to improve your business.

You can't grow if you don't let go.

R&D 1

I want to introduce you to a concept called "R&D"—research and development. A lot of us are self-employed, or in a business where we don't receive leads from the company. We have to learn to research and develop our own contacts.

Now, what we usually do is what I call antenna marketing. We're out somewhere, we're at a function, somebody says something and a little antenna goes up. You say, "Ooh, I better get up there and talk to that person." Well, I want to take you out of antenna marketing. I want to put you into R&D, similar to what would happen if you worked for a big company. You have a sales manager there to ride your butt, making sure you do what you were supposed to do.

First thing we have to do is come up with categories of companies that may potentially use our services. We want to just brainstorm. We're trying to come up with big ideas for right now because we need to think of something that pops in there we haven't really thought about. Let's say I'm a speaker and I want to speak to people that have sales organizations. I'm sitting here and thinking, *OK, who is somebody I could speak to? Insurance companies may have salespeople that I can train.* I go to Google and type in insurance, Alpharetta, Georgia, and some insurance companies appear on the screen.

One of those is American Family. I'm going to make a list starting with American Family. I was thinking about Allstate and State Farm, but I really hadn't thought about American Family. Then there's another one, Nationwide. I'm going to write down Nationwide and then, in this particular way of doing R&D, I want to go through pages two, three, and four on my search results.

Let's go to page two. Let's see what else is coming up. US Auto Insurance and General Insurance. Those are names I normally see going down the street in my village so that's good.

Once you have finished insurance, who else might have salespeople? What about automotive? I go in and type automotive, Alpharetta, Georgia. Auto service at Sears. *Hadn't really thought about Sears, but maybe they train salespeople.* Let's google auto sales. *CarMax, that's a good one.*

Then go to page two of your Google search. I see AutoTrader on there. *I didn't think about that, but I know AutoTrader is online, but maybe they have salespeople that go out and sell to the car dealers.* I might enter attorneys or CPAs. I might add restaurants. What about hair salons and IT companies?

So just think about generic categories. Start brainstorming and start with the letter A. Label it Automotive. B could be for book sales. C is for car dealers, D maybe for dentists. And go through that in your mind to start coming up with as many categories as you can. Write down as many names of potential companies you need to be familiar with. Every time I've done that with coaching clients, names of businesses start popping up in their community they had just forgotten about. They're out of sight, out of mind.

So, the first thing you want to do is create alphabetical categories. That's the first part of your research. Categorize the types of companies that potentially can use your business.

After being in the mortgage business for fifteen years, I decided to write a book. It all started when my mortgage company started to grow unexpectedly. The market was changing and a lot of loan officers at banks were starting to hear that the rules were going to change and a lot of them decided to move to mortgage brokers. Around 2007, my loan-officer count went from about five to twenty-five. I realized most of my new loan officers had depended on bank referrals and that our business was all referral-based. I knew I was going to have to teach the new guys referral-based marketing. I put together a list of some of my ideas and presented it to two fellow mortgage-broker friends at a conference. They loved what I had written and suggested I write a book. Then the 2009 crash came and my business decreased by 90 percent. It was during this time I wrote the book and started thinking I needed to get out on the road and promote my books and speaking business. I realized I needed a way to come up with potential targets for speaking I was not used to calling on. Hence, I came up with the R&D approach. I used this to launch my career as an author and speaker, so I know it works!

R&D 2

I've told you we needed to do our research and development in order to figure out who our best customers are. What I'm going to do now in "R&D 2," is show you how (once you've decided the types of companies you need to go see) to find specific potential customers within them on the internet. We're going to start off with what we learned in "R&D 1." Let's assume we're a financial advisor, and we know doctors make a lot of money so we want to meet more physicians because we want to manage their money. I'm going to my best friend, Google. Let's google orthopedic surgeon, Alpharetta, Georgia, as we did in the previous chapter.

Now, I click on Peachtree Orthopedic. I don't know anybody there, but let's go to their website. Let's assume that a lot of my customers, as a financial advisor, are fifty-five to eighty-five years old and they're getting shoulder surgeries done. So, I go and type in "shoulder surgery." Now it tells me about the physicians at this particular practice. All of these physicians specialize in shoulder surgery, and they would be great people for me to introduce my customers to. Let's pick this doctor named Scott. So, select Scott and it actually has his biography on there. So now I can learn a little bit about Scott. This is important information.

He's been with them since 2008. We find that he is the team physician for the Atlanta Silverbacks, who are a minor-league soccer team. If I know anyone who's heavily involved with soccer in the Atlanta area, there's a good chance they may know someone involved with the Silverbacks. He's also a team physician for Georgia State University. He handles the women's soccer, basketball, and volleyball teams. Well, if I knew anybody that goes to college there, they would know a professor. I might know someone's kid who went there and played one of those sports.

If I do, some of those people can introduce him to me. Now look at his education and training, it tells me he went to University of Georgia. I might know someone at University of Georgia who may have been in his fraternity. It says he also went to Emory University. Also, he attended Westminster High School, which is a pretty prominent high school here in Atlanta. I may know someone who's a teacher at Westminster. I might know some kids or some people my age who went to school there who might know him. It also says he's a family man. He's got three kids.

I can just learn a lot about this particular doctor in case someone I know knows him through one of these different organizations he's been involved with.

So think about going into people's web pages. Once you've picked something in particular—in this case, orthopedic surgeons—go deep. They're at the same practice. And I guarantee you, if I went through every one of those doctors, you're going to come up with something in common. That will allow you to call a friend who may know them and give you an introduction. And of course, the main reason behind the introduction is to bring your assets. "Hey, Dr. Scott, as a financial advisor, I have a lot of customers that could be patients of yours. They're getting shoulder surgeries and knee replacements. I want a good doctor to refer them to." So, that's how you can get into that category.

Now go check the next category.

Let's also say we want to research something fun because part of meeting people and getting referrals is giving referrals out. Somebody called me the other day and said they needed a Santa Claus. I go in and search for "Santa Claus, Roswell, Georgia," in Google because I want to give a referral, and we get a few results.

There's a Santa Claus in Roswell and his name is Thomas Tolbert. We see an article, "One of the Best 11 Santa Clauses in the United States." This was written in New Jersey and he's from Roswell, Georgia. How about that? Now go to Facebook and type in Thomas Tolbert, and there's Santa Claus. He's got a Facebook page. I can look at his friends. We've got 151 mutual friends. Any of those mutual friends have a chance to introduce me to Santa Claus. So, if I don't know Santa Claus, I can try to reach out to my friends to see if they will introduce me to Santa Claus.

And then I get him on the phone and I'm bringing an asset to him. "Hey, Santa, I got a friend of mine who needs someone to be Santa Claus at a party. Would you like for me to have her call you?" Santa is probably going to say he would love to talk to her.

So now you've got the company name, you've got a contact person at the company, and you've done your research to find out who knows that person. You're 50 percent to 75 percent on your way to meeting that person. So, all you have to think about now is, *I've got somebody with a rifle approach, not a shotgun approach. I've zeroed in. And I know if I can get to that person, and have a conversation with them, then there's a really good chance there might be some business that comes out of this.* So focus on making sure you've got the names of a particular person beside each company and go through all your lists we built in "R&D 1." We will learn in "R&D 3" how we go forward and meet those people.

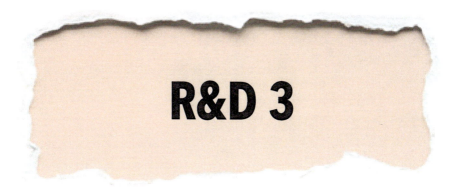

R&D 3

We decided on a category, and we decided on people within that category we wanted to meet. Now that we found the person we want to meet, we're going to do a little bit more research.

Remember, we have to do our research in order to develop that relationship. So let's say I'm looking for someone that does SEO or someone who does video (like Greg is doing for me). I've picked Greg as someone to search for. I searched SEO and one result was Greg Bennett. So, how do I get closer to Greg Bennett? One of the things we discussed is "Circle the Wagons"; this is one part of that.

If I go to Facebook and I type in Greg Bennett, there he is. And so now while I'm there, I can do some research; who his friends are. We start going through there to figure out if we know any of the same people. We can read a little bit about him. I'm trying to find out if there's anybody else I know that he knows. We can also go on LinkedIn. We can come here and see if we have mutual friends.

Greg Bennett might be listed as Greg Bennett Sr. Let's assume it was this guy. Then, when Greg Bennett shows up, we can see if we have any mutual friends. This is how we're connected. These are my friends who know this guy. And so now we'll use that as a way to try to get to Greg Bennett, so you have a chance to develop a relationship with them. And what we want to do is get a lot more specific about people in the community or people in our world who could possibly change our lives.

Most of us don't do this kind of deep research. I usually do this on a Saturday or Sunday when there's nobody around. I turn on some music and I go through and start researching and coming up with all kinds of different people for me to start working on, to start meeting so I could start developing a relationship with. So that's "R&D 3"!

A FEW BIG IDEAS

R&D 4

The next thing is put the names on a big sticky pad listed by companies and the person you want to meet at that particular company. I usually come in on Saturdays, and I start looking for companies I could go speak to.

Here's the cool thing about the big sticky pads. If you put these sticky notes up, you're looking at this the same way a customer would look at them if you came to my office. And so, people will sit there while we're talking, and they'll look up on the wall and say, "What's that about?"

And I say, "Well, I'm trying to meet somebody at Price Waterhouse, but I don't know anybody there."

And they'll say, "Well, I know a friend there. My sister works there." And often I get them to give me a lead or a referral to get to that company because I'm kind of advertising who I'm going after.

It also gives me a chance to tell them why I've got that up there. So, once you isolate the companies, you need to put them in a prominent place where people come into your office. You never know, the person in the cubicle next door may know somebody at one of those companies. You've just never asked them.

So, use this sticky pad system. And once you've met all those people, you create a whole new group of people. It might take me a year to go through those people or it might take me a month. Depends on how aggressive I want to be in getting out there and trying to grow my speaking business. You're trying to meet a person within that category or that company. Categories, to companies, to a person, then trying to meet them.

Passions

Everybody has a passion. It might be their hobby, a nonprofit, or their grandkids. Most people go to work thinking about closing time so they can go do the things they are passionate about. If you really want to connect with someone on a deeper level, then connect with them on their passion. Spend some time each day calling your friends and customers and just learn about their passions. Write down their passion in their contact information on your phone. Find some way to record it so you have an excuse to call them about it. When you write it down, it will be searchable when you need it.

People love to talk about their passions, and you can always have a reason to call them to discuss it. "Hey, Jim, how is your training for the marathon going?"

"Hey, Jane, last time we spoke you were taking the grandkids to Disney World, how did that go?"

I have a few friends who love flying. Most of them own small planes. When I see a plane or take a flight with one of them, it gives me an excuse to call the others and talk about my flight. Pilots love to talk about other planes and flying!

Several of my friends have cool cars. Some have Ferraris and some have old trucks or antique cars. When I see one on the road or in someone's garage, I use that as a reason to call the other motorheads to tell them about it.

As salespeople, we are always looking for a reason to reach out to customers. Knowing their passions/hobbies is the perfect reason.

People like you more when they know you understand what's important to them.

I met a guy named Ron Clark who was speaking at my Rotary Club. I heard about him through my wife because she had heard his story on Oprah. To say this guy is passionate about education would be an understatement. He was eaten up with it. Over the years, I have found that if I meet someone passionate about a project, then I want to help them fulfill it. So, I jumped in to help Ron Clark start a school. I introduced him to everyone I could. I helped him market to schoolteachers and principals. I volunteered at the school and gave him money. Today it is one of the best schools in America. I had a small part but what is exciting is to see his passion come together and to see how many people around the globe he has touched. If you meet someone that is on fire with passion, jump in and help. See chapter on "Life Purpose."

Increase Your Prices

Several years ago, I heard a guy speak at a business meeting about how he bought companies where he could increase the prices. He wanted to increase the prices and hold onto the top 20 percent of customers and fire the bottom 20 percent. He said the bottom 20 percent were problem children who drained your time and resources. He then pulled out a chart that blew me away.

If you own a men's clothing store, you probably mark up everything 50 percent or what they call "keystone." A shirt costs you twenty-five dollars and you sell it for fifty dollars. But here is the kicker. If you put the shirts on sale at a 25 percent discount, you have to sell 100 percent more shirts to make the original profit. So, if you have fifty shirts you discount at 25 percent off, you need to sell one hundred shirts to make up the discount.

However, if you take those same shirts and increase the price 20 percent more, you can sell 28 percent less shirts. You don't have to service as many customers to make the same money.

After seeing this, I stopped chasing customers because I wanted to do more lucrative deals. I started chasing good customers who value what I bring to the table and not just people looking for a deal. The deal seekers only send other deal seekers. The relationship-customer and service-oriented customers send more like themselves. That's who I want!

This not only gave me more time to support the great customers, it also created more good customers and increased my profits. I dare you to do this because it works and you'll have more time for your family and referral sources.

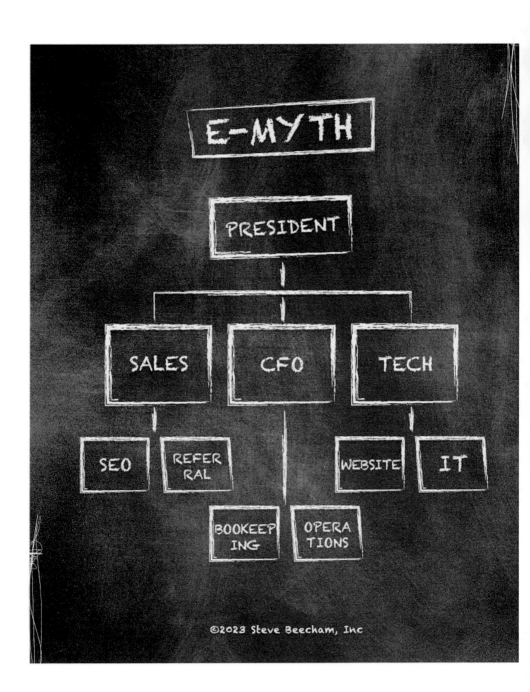

Hiring

Here is how you should plan to hire and build out your organization over the next couple of years. I got this idea from reading.

Pull out a blank sheet of paper and draw a box near the top of the page in the center. Then write your name in the box and put CEO under it. Draw two boxes directly under that box. Write sales in one box and CFO in the other one. You are creating an inverse pyramid of boxes. Your name may appear in all the boxes if you are a one-man operation. But, if you want to build a company you need to lay out all the boxes that everyone would do if it was a perfectly well-oiled machine. Your job is to hire people to fill the boxes over time and each hire takes responsibility away from you. [1]

When hiring people, think about a football team. Each person has a specific duty. It works the same way at Wendy's. One person handles french fries and another person handles the cash register. In football, one player blocks and another player runs with the ball. You want to fill the box very specifically so understanding the job description is very important. If the potential person doesn't have the right set of tools, keep looking.

Then think about the culture you want to create or already have. What are the three common elements that people MUST have to work here? If they don't have the main three, you don't hire.

If you are not a social person, don't like to post on social media, and go to parties or functions, you won't make it here at Home Town Mortgage. Why? Because my son and I like that and we are built around the idea of getting out, knowing, and loving on people. You have a culture too. It does not have to be like mine, but the people you hire need to fit in easily.

---

[1] Constance Moonzwe, "How to Build Your Company Organization Chart," Meet Constance, September 13, 2017, https://www.meetconstance.com/blog/2017/9/13/organization-chart.

I Believe

Do you believe you should be the person people call? Do you believe you know as much about your craft as anyone else? Do you believe others are messing up by not using you?

You need to believe these things. Belief in your abilities is key to becoming the dominant player in your category. Practice believing.

When you believe, you start to motivate yourself. That motivation makes you go out and talk to others. It makes you want to learn more about your craft. You face your fears instead of running from them. You talk to yourself in a positive, upbeat, affirmative kind of way. You increase your confidence in yourself.

You have to believe you are the go-to person. You will have problems and issues you don't know how to handle, but if you believe in yourself, you will find a way to get the right answer and you will never have that deficit again.

BELIEFS turn to THOUGHTS which shape your FEELINGS.

It's called Cognitive Behavior. The triangle is where you want to be. It elevates you and holds you personally accountable for your beliefs, thoughts, and feelings.

My brother Stan, a sports psychologist, was working with a professional golfer. He asked her what was going on and she said she was struggling with putting. She was in the top ten in driving and chipping but not in putting. So, they went to the putting green and he put a ball down as far away from the cup as he could. He then asked her to putt it in. As she came back on her backstroke, he grabbed the club and said to her, "What are you thinking?"

She said, "I can't make the putt from here so I am focusing on getting it as close to the hole as possible and leaving it on the left side which would make it an easy tap in."

Stan, then said, "So you don't believe you can make that putt?"

"No," she said.

He talked to her about how she had been putting since she was a child just like she had been driving and chipping. He brought to her attention that the problem wasn't her bad putting, but that she didn't BELIEVE she could make the putt. He told her she had a BELIEF problem, not a putting problem. She believed she could drive the ball or chip it where it needed to be but didn't BELIEVE she could putt the ball in. Stan mentioned that the last time he checked, the one who made the fewest strokes won. She just needed to BELIEVE she was good enough to putt it in!

Mentoring : The Greatest Way to Give Back Your Knowledge

Have you thought about mentoring people in your community? I didn't realize the power of mentoring until recently. I started coaching people and they would say, "Hey, my friend needs some help, would you sit down with them, Beech?" Then, some parents started bringing their kids to talk with me. I started doing some speaking in colleges and realized that those minds of mush really need a mentor.

I need and seek out mentors. Mentoring others has made me more aware that I need to seek out advice from others too. Mentorship is a two-way street. You give others some of what you know, and others give you some of what they know. When you engage in mentoring, it changes the perception of you in your community. People see you as a giving, caring person, not just as a businessperson. They see you as an individual trying to get better at their craft, not just trying to make a sale.

High School Students

Start thinking about opportunities to mentor. Almost every high school has an FBLA (Future Business Leaders of America), or some sort of business group. Those teachers are looking for opportunities to have those kids mentored. The teachers will help you get plugged in by either speaking to the group, hiring a student, or doing a one-on-one mentoring session with a student who has an interest in your area of expertise. Reach out to your local high school and ask if they need any help. You might just show up at school and help with a business day, or you might come in and do a speech. When you take some kids and mentor them a little bit, the word gets out in the school. The kid goes back and tells their parents. "Man, Steve helped me with this," or "Steve told me what I need to do to be successful. He came and spoke to our class and sat down and explained how this works to me." That's the kind of vibe you want in the community and that builds good BUZZ!

College Students

If I'm talking to someone and they tell me their child is thinking about getting into the financial business, I tell them that's the business I'm in. I let them know I'd love to talk to them. I can teach them what I know about the financial business, not just the mortgage side, but maybe the stocks and bonds, bank-type stuff. I encourage them to get their student to come over to my house and bring their notebook and we'll sit down and talk about the financial business and all the aspects associated with it since I know a lot about it and know a lot of people. I could refer them for future jobs. I let them know that's what I did with my kids because they don't want to listen to me but will listen to others and I will be that other person for you!

When you are mentoring a college student, it is important to introduce them to other mentors in the exact field they have a current interest in. You must find that person for them. They are, for whatever reason, hyper-focused on a certain career, and they need your help in learning as much as they can so they can make a good decision on that career. They will go back to their parents and friends and tell them how helpful and connected you are, which is great BUZZ for you!

Business Owners

Be the person in the community that's there to mentor new business owners. If you're a successful businessperson, be that person. Let people know at the chamber of commerce, let people know at city hall that if somebody is trying to start a business, you'd be happy to help them. If you're good at what you do, you don't mind mentoring people. The reason is you're not scared the other person's going to steal your ideas or your customers. That's what I find with highly successful people. That's why they don't mind mentoring. If you're good at what you do, look for opportunities to mentor other businesspeople. It's a great way to get really good Buzz in the community, and for other people to know you really are a great person, that you really care about other people. That's how you get more business!

Let me tell you about the time I got mentored. The community development director called a meeting of some people to talk about redevelopment of our downtown. I was the youngest and least knowledgeable about community development, but she thought it would be good to have me since I was a local downtown business and a landowner. The group had a land planner and several developers in the group. All of these guys were legends in their field. For the next year, we met and came up with a plan. A plan to totally redevelop and reconfigure how our town looked. It was a lesson in city government and land-use planning. I loved it and met some great people. The best part is I learned how to look at large-scale projects from the experts. I learned how they figured out cost and how they assessed what might work. Their process was totally different than what I knew at that point and because of them, I changed how I ran my business. The moral of the story is people who are smarter and wiser can bring you value even if they are in a different field of work.

Praise

Praise someone who has done you a favor.

Send their boss a letter. Send their spouse or kids a letter. Let them know how much you appreciate them sending you a referral.

I want my roses Now! Don't wait until it's too late to tell someone how much you appreciate them.

My wife received this letter recently:

Dear Mary,

Thank you so much for being your husband's biggest cheerleader and support team. Because of your support, Steve is able to impact mortgage lenders all over the nation. Steve has been such a blessing to me in my speaking and business. I just want to take a minute and thank the person behind the scenes.

Sincerely,
Mark Bradley

Send your roses when they happen. Show your heart and your feelings now, not at their funeral.

And make it a hand-written note. People love getting handwritten notes. I know it's a bit old-fashioned but, it shows you care. If you want to make it more impactful, include a Starbucks or Chick-fil-A gift card.

When Mark gets a referral, he sends a handwritten thank-you note. He thanks them for the referral and includes either a gift card or a book that would be of interest to them. One of his referral-givers, who loves the Georgia Bulldogs, received a thank-you note with a copy of a Vince Dooley book.

Mini Me

Napoleon Hill introduced this to me in his book *Think and Grow Rich*. I use this concept a lot!

If you get an appointment with someone, use this concept. It may be a sales call, a phone appointment, or a visit with a current customer. Send in your Mini Me.

Your Mini Me is your alter ego.

It is you but with a different name. They look and talk and act just like you, but they are make-believe.

I call my Mini Me "Beech." In my mind, Beech will have a conversation with the other person I am going to meet. When Beech visits this person, he's going to say, "I know you're going to be talking to Beech tomorrow. He's a great guy." I then make up all kinds of stuff to talk about myself to this other person.

I might ask them what are some of your questions and concerns about Beech? I have that conversation in my mind before I have the actual conversation with this person. The great thing about that is it will help prepare you for your talk with that person. It'll also help you get more pumped up about going in and talking to somebody. Pumped up about talking about the great things that you bring to the table.

Next time you've got an appointment, before you physically go, send in your Mini Me the day before or the hour before and let your Mini Me have a conversation with that person. I guarantee it'll help you when you get there, and you'll have more sales when you send your Mini Me.

It basically works for anything. Sometimes I send my Mini Me to clear the traffic when I am running late or looking for a parking spot at the mall. I even use him when I am about to call someone for a favor like a concert ticket or money for a charity.

Fear

Napoleon Hill said, "Fear is just not knowing the answer to a question." That was huge for me. He is so right. If someone is about to push you off a cliff, you have fear because you don't know if they will or not. You don't know if you will die or not. But if you found out they were just playing and you stepped back away from the cliff, you no longer have fear. Life is like that. We get scared when we don't know what the outcome will be.

So how do we solve that? By tasking it out. Take an issue like, "I won't be able to pay my mortgage next month because I do not have enough business." Then, task out what I would need to do to make that different.

Get a customer. How?

- Start calling my old customers and see if they know anyone who could use my services.
- Post an ad on social media that is free.
- Go to a meeting where potential customers might be.
- Find a bunch of people I can help get more customers—because if I help enough people, they will help me.
- Borrow money from someone.
- Call my parents or siblings.
- Pawn my car, guns, or jewelry.
- Call my banker to get a line of credit against my house.
- Sell something of value.
- List my house.
- Go through the basement and put stuff on Facebook Marketplace.

- Fill business pipeline.
- Start with "A–Z" or "Top 100." Call as many people in your database, including past clients. Use "FORD" scripting.
- Use the "Spoke and Hub" system. If you are an insurance or real estate agent and you work on the north side of town, start calling people in your industry on the south side of town and explain how you will refer business to them.
- Look at the chapter on "Create Your Own Club." Start a networking meeting at Waffle House.

When you task it out, it gives you options and eliminates some of the fear. Once you write it down, you can begin to put together a game plan for how to eliminate your fear.

In other words, FOCUS on solutions and not on the problem. The answers give you strength.

Bottles and Brainstorming

If you go to an event and you meet some cool people, give someone else some advice and others help you with ideas to solve an issue, then you have been to the perfect event. I thought up this idea after going to networking events for forty years.

It's called "Bottles and Brainstorming." We will sample some really good adult beverages during each break.

We invite all our business friends to come to an event to help them with issues. Some are personal and some are business. Most of the invitees are in sales or own a small business. We gather in small groups narrated by a guru and discuss our issues pertaining to the guru's expertise. While in the small group, participants can add value to the discussion and sometimes you get value from the group. The gurus are not there to preach or to tell you what to do, but to facilitate a discussion about an issue someone in the group is experiencing. This is important because you are there to help others in an area you are knowledgeable. We want people to leave the evening feeling like they gave some knowledge, received some knowledge, and met new people. Kind of the triple crown of a great networking evening.

The evening will start with a tasting and then an introduction of the gurus. Each guru will have a table or area with eight to ten seats around them, much like a small-group Bible study. Participants will meet in each small group for thirty minutes and then we will taste another beverage. Then go to the next small group. Participants will get to go to three different groups in two hours. We should have fifty to sixty people, so not everyone will get to every group.

People love this event because they get to give some knowledge, receive some knowledge, and meet a lot of new cool people because they are in small groups.

Board of Directors

Who do you work for? For most of us, it is our family.

The important thing to remember is *you* work for *them*. They own part of the experience.

I sat down with my young family and told them they all owned 20 percent of Home Town Mortgage. They were eight to thirteen years old at the time. They said WOW!

I explained to them as an owner/board member, I needed their input since they could hire or fire me and they were responsible for how much I got paid.

I explained to them how my business worked and how I received business. I explained to them the money the company earned was used to pay for things like the food we are eating and their football and softball cleats. It paid for a beach vacation each summer and that the more money Home Town made, the more smoothies they could have and the more camps they could go to.

I explained that I needed their input on how I spent my time. Should I take the call from the real estate agent if I was watching their game or we were out playing?

They all agreed I should take the call. They wanted more motorcycles and four-wheelers and trips. Do this with your family so you have their blessings when you work and when you play.

You need to do the same, so you won't feel bad about not spending quality time with your family. When I think of how I manage my time, I refer back to what the board would want me to do. All my decisions are made based on what the board wants me to do.

After you do this, you can then get mentors to help you with business decisions.

After dinner one night, my youngest son, Colin, wanted to call a board meeting. He indicated he had outgrown his 50cc mini-bike and he wanted an 80cc dirt bike with a clutch. He wanted to know if there was anything he could do to help Home Town Mortgage make more money so he could get a new dirt bike. I told him that if he could get me two loans, we would have enough money to get him a dirt bike. Colin told me that none of his eleven-year-old buddies were buying houses. I told him he needed to be an FBI agent and that if he overheard any of his buddies' parents talking about finishing their basement or wanting to buy a vacation home, to let me know. A month later, he got a new dirt bike.

Go Pro in Your Sport

If you want to go to the Pro Bowl, you have to do things differently than everyone else. Pro Bowlers work on different techniques. They study their sport, not just play it.

Start looking 360 degrees around you. Who do you touch in your day-to-day activities? In the mortgage business, we touch real estate agents, appraisers, closing attorneys, and surveyors. In the financial advisor sector, you could go visit the New York Stock Exchange, Mercantile Exchange in Chicago, or visit estate attorneys. You should spend some time with each of them, learning about their craft. If you do, you will be smarter than any other mortgage person. Look around you and see who you send business to and who sends business to you and start asking them a lot of questions.

Books are great to dive deeper into what you do. Are you reading books about sales and psychology? Are you learning all about your industry and reading about others who have become successful doing what you do?

When was the last time you went to an industry seminar and paid to hear an industry guru speak? Go! Only the top players do that.

If there is a mentoring or coaching program within your company, take advantage of that.

Mirror someone who is already successful.

Learn about time management and how you can create more family time and how you can prospect better. You have it down when you can teach others how to do that better.

Invent something in your sport. Be the only one who has

thought about how to make it cheaper, faster, or better. Come up with your own invention and tell your customers you did. It will let them know you are all in on getting better and making it better for your customers.

Jerry Rice is the perfect example of Going Pro. He worked year-round when it was not the norm in pro sports. He did things beyond football practice. He took ballet, ran up sand dunes, flipped tires.

So, if you want to go deep in your field, do the things others are not doing or willing to do. Be different and unconventional.

People love this event because they get to give some knowledge, receive some knowledge, and meet a lot of new cool people because they are in small groups.

⭐ TOP 100 – FOR LIFE ⭐

ZAC BROWN
TED TURNER ⭐
KIRDY
DABO
TOM COUSINS
JAMES CORDON
SADGURU
~~DAN CATHY~~
ELON
TRUMP JR
ADAM GRANT
JENNY PRUITT
LIL ALLEYS OWNER
BRENE BROWN
~~MARK SPAIN~~
TONY ROBBINS

DALI LAMA
ED BASTION
SARA BLAKELY
~~STEPHANIE STUCKEY~~
ANDRE DICKENS
⭐B JEFFREY GRIBBLE
HURRICANE HANNAH
ARTHUR BLANK
~~VINCE DOOLEY~~
CHUCK LEAVELL
TYLER PERRY
ALEX TAYLOR
RON DESANTIS
SMITH & KENNEDY
E CRAFT HOMES
⭐ELTON JOHN

©2023 Steve Beecham, Inc

Top 100 – For Life

Same principle as "Top 100" but these are people who are game changers. People you would love to meet before you die. People like Oprah Winfrey, Tony Robbins, Elon Musk, the Dali Lama, the Pope, Adam Grant, and Brene Brown.

These are people you would love to have a cup of coffee with and really get to know more about how they became successful and what their secrets are.

I started this list and I have been surprised by how many of the people I have been able to check off the list. Now, all my people are not rock stars. A lot of them are local rock stars. People I have read about in the paper or have known about through others.

Probably the most interesting part of doing this is having other people see the list. I have them on a chalkboard behind my desk. Everyone who walks into my office asks about the list and a lot of them mention they know one of the people and know how to get me in front of one of them. But better yet, it gives me a little BUZZ with them. Can't you just hear them telling someone else about my list and what a great idea it is?

Here is my current list of people I have not met. If you can introduce me, I would love to have a cup of coffee with these folks or have them on my podcast.

Who would you put on your list?

Write down *your* Top 100 – For Life in the notes section at the end of this book.

Make It Happen

Don't wait for it to happen. A lot of folks are not going to get this marketing idea, but it may be one of the best, most enjoyable things I do.

I believe that Napoleon Hill was right when he said, "This world belongs to those who take possession of it and make things happen."

People talk about people who make things happen. The person who opens a new store or restaurant. The guy who drives the cool car to the ball games on Saturday. The lady who built the most gorgeous home in the neighborhood.

Be that person in your village.

One night after dinner, Mary and I were sitting on a park bench in downtown Alpharetta. It was about nine p.m. and the town was dead. The restaurants were closing up and nobody was walking around on a beautiful spring night. We thought that was a shame. I wondered what we could do about it. Mary said if we had live music, maybe people would stay out a little longer. I decided to make it happen.

The problem was I wanted to do it in downtown on the City Green and the City Springs, which would tear up the grass and change it to turf the next month. Additionally, the city had never let anyone do anything on the City Green because it was a public space for all. But a friend of mine knew the answer. My friend Janet knew I could get a restaurant to let me put the stage on their property and point the stage to the green and then everyone could sit on the green and the band would be on private property. Chiringa, a local restaurant next to the green, agreed to go in on the concerts. Next, I had to find a band. So, I tapped into my local network of buddies and started looking for local garage bands who would play cheap but love the exposure. Then, I had to find a stage, lights, and sound. The cost ended up being about two thousand per concert and now I had to call my business friends to see if they would help pay for it. If they did, I would put up a banner for advertising on their behalf.

To say it went well is an understatement. We had two hundred to five hundred people show up for the concerts over the summer. We then expanded and brought in a big-screen TV for Saturday football games and we had the town rocking in the evenings. As of this writing, we are planning our third summer concert series and the city found a way to let me actually be on the green by making it a community event.

But here is the cool part. While the concerts are going on, I get to walk around the crowd and ask perfect strangers if they are enjoying it, what kind of music they like, and where they are from or where they live in the community. They look at me kind of funny and say, "Are you responsible?" I tell them I am and they always say thank you for doing this and ask for my name and what I do. And then I get to tell them.

Also, my friends will bring their friends up to me and say, "I want you to meet Steve, he is the guy putting this on."

To say I have gotten some BUZZ out of this is an understatement!

Prior to Covid, I started getting this feeling that people need a different kind of way to meet other businesspeople. I have been to a ton of networking events and because I have young-adult children now in the workforce, I felt like there was a need for some coaching or mentoring. Since I am in the speaking and writing business, and spend some time in a group called Vistage, I know a lot of folks who are really good at what they do. I put together a brainstorming event with some business Guru's. The event was a huge success and you can read about it in the chapter titled "Bottles and Brainstorming." There was a need and I made it happen for my community. Now people know if they need expert advice, I can help or know someone who can. Young adults know that mature businesspeople are willing to give them their knowledge.

Many years ago, I was involved in the North Fulton Chamber and even sat on the board. During that time, in the 1980s, North Fulton County was quickly growing. We had so many people moving to our area who were not from around there—a lot of out-of-state people. They would always ask questions about why there weren't any sewers over here, or why there were county but not city police. I decided we needed a program to educate people about the area and put together the framework and idea of what became Leadership North Fulton. The idea was to introduce people to city and county officials and all the major employers in the area. At the same time, they had the opportunity to network and build new friendships with other chamber members. The program took off with the help of some very talented people and now most of the chambers in my area do a similar program.

I joined the Alpharetta Rotary Club when there were only about thirty members, and they were in their second year. That was over thirty years ago! We now have over 150 members, and we are one of the best clubs in the country—very diverse in age, gender, and race. After I wrote my first book, I went around to Rotary Clubs speaking. It gave me great incite as to what clubs were successful and which ones were not. One of the things I noticed was that great clubs had all the players in the club. They had the mayor, parks and recreation director, the police chief, and the fire chief. The Alpharetta club did not. If you have those people in your club, you can make things happen—like setting up a parade very quickly, or any fundraising event you want to do. I felt like that was what the Alpharetta club needed and proposed the idea that the mayor, police, and the fire chief should all be honorary members. The club agreed and because of that, our growth took off. I just recently got the state representative and senator to be honorary members too. Why is this important? When you bring a prospective member to our club, and you introduce him to the guy who will fix his pothole, the guy who will fix his speeding ticket, and the guy who will bring the fire truck by for his kid's birthday party, he or she gets pretty excited. When the club wants to have a fundraiser and one of your members can make that happen on the spot, stuff gets done quickly.

Successful people don't wait for something to happen, they go make it happen. You need to do the same in your community. When you do, it creates BUZZ about you and your business.

Top 100 Notes

Top 100 – For Life Notes

About the Author

Steve Beecham is a speaker and author specializing in helping companies and individuals grow their businesses by leveraging professional and social connections more effectively. Steve has authored three books that drive home the messages in his seminars and corporate presentations. *Bass-Ackwards Business: The Power of Helping Without Hustling*, is about building deeper relationships and painting better pictures for the people in your village so when they think about your industry, they think of you first. His second book, *What's Your Buzz?*, is about understanding what is being said about you and your business, and how to use it to your advantage. In his most recent book, *The Tapes We Play in Our Head*, Steve helps readers identify negative self-talk and turn it into positive and inspiring messages.

Beecham started his career in the retail industry as the owner of an upscale clothing store in his hometown of Roswell, Georgia. Several years later, at the suggestion of a friend, Steve gave the mortgage business a try, and after realizing quick success, opened Home Town Mortgage in Alpharetta, Georgia. During his twenty-five years running his own mortgage company, Steve has interviewed hundreds of top salespeople and identified what he feels are the common elements of success. Through trial and error, he developed his remarkable system of helping people while not hustling them for business, making him what many call "the mayor of his village." Beecham says he has spent years working for his perfect scenario: "My phone rings and people ask to spend money with me."

An engaging and entertaining speaker and storyteller, Steve has spoken to sales and marketing professionals at companies across the country, including Edward Jones, Merrill Lynch, Travelers, Prudential Financial, John Hancock, Mass Mutual, Wells Fargo, Country Financial, Allstate, State Farm, Nationwide, Comcast, Seyfarth and Shaw, Global Healthcare, Cole Publishing, the University of Georgia, and Kennesaw State University, sharing strategies and techniques for growing referral business.

Beecham has served on the boards of the Ron Clark Academy, North Fulton Community Charities, the Alpharetta Public Safety Foundation, Alpharetta Rotary, and Wellstar North Fulton Hospital, and is currently on the board at Meals By Grace in Cumming, Georgia. He is featured in *How to Win Friends and Influence People in the Digital Age*, the modern adaptation of the bestselling personal growth book of all time by Dale Carnegie.

Learn more about Steve at www.stevebeecham.com.

About the Contributor

Mark Bradley is a CEO and business coach in the real-estate industry. He has spent twenty-two years selling homes to his clients and being awarded as a top producer in the Atlanta area. In 2009, he received his broker's license and started coaching and training agents throughout the area. His philosophy is to provide clients with service that exceed their expectations. He slowly grows into a servant leadership role at whatever organization he is associated with.

Having owned and operated three different business ventures, he came to realize we are all in the people business. While the first venture didn't work out as planned, it taught him several lessons about how you treat people. If you get to know them on a personal level, you will succeed in your business. And it's not just about business, it's about having a personal relationship with someone you honestly care about.

He has a BA in public relations with minor degrees in journalism and marketing. He has been published in several magazine articles over the years and was a staff writer at a local newspaper. Mark has also been involved in several charity and volunteer organizations over the years with most of the focus on helping kids.

Other Books by Steve Beecham

*Bass-Ackward Business:
The Power of Helping
without Hustling*

*What's Your Buzz?:
Finding and Creating the Right Talk about You
and Your Business*

*The Tapes We Play in Our Head: How to Have More
Powerful Conversations
with Yourself*